MW01290564

In 2008, Donald Charles Davis, as *The Aging Rebel,* began writing news reports, essays and reviews aimed at an audience of motorcycle outlaws. The 50 selections in this book were originally published on the web at www.agingrebel.com. They provide a general audience with a candid look at the motorcycle outlaw world.

At forty two seconds, just outside the front door, John Lindeman dies. He dies. I know he dies. I have seen men die. So, I recognize that Lindeman has died. Even if I had not seen men die I would see that Ripley Lindeman died beautifully. He died beautifully as the Loyalist Militiaman died beautifully in Robert Capa's classic photograph, "The Falling Soldier:" Falling, spinning, elegant, brave, poetically doomed. Except Capa's photograph was a fraud and Lindeman really died. What I cannot tell is whether Lindeman died after he hit the ground or before.

The Aging Rebel:

Dispatches From The Motorcycle Outlaw Frontier

Donald Charles Davis

Copyright © 2008 - 2011 Donald Charles Davis
All rights reserved.
ISBN: 10: 146796011X
ISBN-13: 978-1467960113

Contents

The Rebel Rides 1

Angel Walks Into A Bar 5

County Bans Screaming Orgasm 8

Methland 12

Framing Dave Burgess 21

Dave Burgess' Appeal 45

Dave Burgess And BALCO 48

Arizona Citizen Snaps 57

Great Basin Highway 61

Deadly And Delicious 70

Bikers Still Menace 73

Sioux Falls Defense Rests 77

HA Trademark Suit 82

Hi Yo Silver 86

Lancaster Boots Mongols 89

Lars Wilson Flipped 92

East LA Saturday Night 95

Special Memory Knife Fight 97

Whores Will Save Vegas 99

Chosen Few Week 27 105

Mark Walker Arrested 110

Myrtle Beach Warns You 113

Myrtle Beach Laugh Riot 116

Tweeting Incarceration 119
Stahlman Trial Begins 122
Hugh Harrison "Harry" Hurt 125
Railroad Tie Kills Rider 132
"Tommy Gun" Martinez 135
Max Joseph Aragon 136
James Alan "Wolf" Corrao 138
Property Of John 140
Obama Snubs Rolling Thunder 142
Vung Tau 150
Bruce Rossmeyer 162
Swat Murdered Russell Doza 164
Who The Tulsa Sheriffs Killed 173
The Derringer In Doza's Hand 176
Edge Trap Law Suit 184
Brother Speed Pack Crash 187
Invaders Case In A Nutshell 189
Escape From El Lay 194
Longrider Pauses In Yuma 206
Why James Hicks Died 209
Dulaney Out Of Pagans Case 212
Suppressing Indicia Warrants 215
Shameless Iron Pigs 219
Waiting For SAMCRO Again 222
The Hemet Hoax 232
Watching Lindeman Die 243
The Poker Run 259

The Rebel Rides

I was not my mother's pride and joy. Let that go right there.

My father could never have managed to play a father on TV.

I don't know what my brother who died could have grown up to be.

My sister went to Bible College so now she can speak authoritatively when she states her sincere belief that Jesus sure as Hell did not die to save the likes of me. Also, she is grossly obese. But she doesn't blame it on a glandular disorder like some people might. She thinks being fat is somehow on account of the molestations.

Eventually, by working at jobs he hated, my old man raised his economic status to the point where he actually owned a postage stamp piece of land. He grew rocks and tree stumps for the most part. And my job in the family was to dig them out for him. Sometimes, when I did a particularly good job he gave me a half a can of beer to drink. Other times all I got was constructive criticism.

My father and I were never buddies. We did not play catch. I tried to stay out of his way. But we did have a father-and-son talk when I was 18.

"You're 18-years-old. What are you gonna do? What do you think?" We were walking down the kind of road nobody walks down anymore. It was Spring. The air was buzzing.

I kept waving my hand in front of me. "I don't know. What do you think? The Army or the Marine Corps?"

"The Marine Corps? Why? So you can come home and impress some girl with your pretty dress blues? You're going to hate the Marines. I know you. Let me tell you about chipping paint." He lit a cigarette and shared it with me while he told me about going over the side of a ship and chipping off the old paint. The cigarette timed out how far we were going to walk and it discouraged the bugs. "The Army's not much better."

We started back. The old man lit another cigarette. He was a chain smoker. I didn't want to smoke anymore. This was our first actual talk and I was pretty sure it would be our last. So I wanted to take this golden opportunity to confess to him my most secret ambition. "I've been thinking about trying to go to college."

The old man laughed. Then he coughed for about a minute. "Are you drunk? You know you're not smart enough for college. He shook his head. "Geez." He laughed and he coughed some more.

"Then I don't know."

We stopped when we got back to what we used to call our yard. The old man grabbed my arm. "If I was you...." He got close to my face. His breath was hot and smelled like Lucky Strikes. "If I was you I would buy a motorcycle. Hear me? I would buy a motorcycle and I would get the hell out of here." I might not have been smart enough for college but I was smart enough to know that he was talking about himself. He wasn't talking about me. "I would get on that motorcycle and I would just go be free."

So, it was my old man who put the idea in my mind.

Of course, I ignored the son-of-a-bitch for about ten years. I had big plans. I wasn't going to be me. I was going to be somebody better than me. And then all those plans had to be revised. Then my new and improved and smaller plans got revised. Eventually, I got stuck being me.

I did not see my father for years at a stretch. And, we did not have much to say to each other when we did meet. After a while, I started to think every time I saw him would be the last time. The laughs got fewer. The coughing got worse. The signatures on the Christmas cards got shakier.

By then he had already been dead to me most of my life. But, it is never the things you say or do that eat at you. The worst parts of life are always what you did not do or did not say. So I wrote the old man a letter.

"Dear Dad. Remember that advice you gave me that time about getting a motorcycle? Well, I never said thanks and I wanted to thank you for that. Every time I get on my bike I think about thanking you."

This was in the mid-90s. It was about a year before he died. He never bothered to write me back. It was too late for him to live his life through me so why should he? I did not hold it against him. He probably felt about the same way I felt when I did not go to his funeral.

But I did not forget him. In fact, I probably like him more now than I did when he was alive.

And, I do still love to ride my motorcycle. When I ride I still feel 18-years-old and free and all the possibilities of what I might yet do and see and know and what my life might yet be seem to stretch out forever in front of me like a long, grey ribbon of highway. And, I know I have the old-son-of-bitch to thank for that. And, I know that most fathers leave their sons less.

Angel Walks Into A Bar

So, a Hells Angel walks into a crowded bar with a couple of friends and announces he is "taking over." Who among us has not at least thought about doing this? Let him cast the first stone.

Apparently, the notion of such an anti-social outrage has never occurred to Ventura County, California prosecutor Derek Malan. Malan wants to put Brandon Thomas Mundell, 28, a member of the San Fernando Valley Charter of the Hells Angels Motorcycle Club in prison for 11 years and four months for doing basically that.

Mundell, also hit a bar patron in the buttocks with a pool cue causing two welts, "brandished" a four inch knife, and had a blood-alcohol level of .14 percent, which is about double the legal limit to qualify as an intoxicated person in California. The unnamed victims of Mundell's attack were three men who physically tried to prevent Mundell and two associates from entering the Take Five Bar in Newbury Park about 1:30 am on January 19th, 2006.

The Take Five has since gone out of business.

Mundell's two associates were not members of the Hells Angels. There were about 75 to 150 people in

5

the bar at the time of the incident. And, some of them called police to report that "three Hells Angels" were "acting like idiots."

Ventura County Sheriff's Deputy Mark Grambling also suffered several scratches and a bruise on his leg when Mundell accidently hit the Deputy while trying to ride away on his motorcycle. Another cop, Ventura Police Department Officer Michael Brown, has stated that Mundell believed the bar was frequented by members of the Camarillo chapter of the Mongols Motorcycle Club and that he went there hoping that he would be "jumped" by Mongols and so have the opportunity to fight them.

When Mundell was tried last Thursday and Friday jurors were shown about 20 minutes of surveillance video footage of the incident. Much of the footage shows Mundell trying to pick up a woman at the bar. Mundell told the jury that at the time he felt like the "entire bar" was "against him." The one witness to testify on Mundell's behalf was a stripper who said the accused biker is actually very "nice."

Mundell has already pleaded guilty to driving under the influence but he is contesting three counts of assault with a deadly weapon. The prosecutor has also "enhanced" those charges by alleging that Mundell got drunk and acted like an idiot "for the benefit of the Hells Angels."

The "gang enhancement" has given the prosecutor the opportunity to turn Mundell's unfortunate night into a show trial of the Hells Angels Motorcycle Club and the biker way in general.

Malan wanted to show jurors video footage of the great biker brawl of 2002 in Laughlin between members of the Hells Angels and Mongols in Harrah's Casino but was denied by Ventura County Superior Court Judge Kevin DeNoce. The judge did, however, allow testimony about the Laughlin brawl and about the Hells Angels.

So jurors heard from a "gang expert," Ventura County Sheriff's Department Deputy Jeremy Paris.

Paris told jurors that that his "gang intelligence" indicated that the Angels were worried that the club's "image is suffering in the media" and the club is encouraging members to do "more charity fundraisers, especially those that would benefit families." Apparently, Paris thinks this is mendacious in some way.

Paris also testified that the Hells Angels are a "violent criminal organization." But then, what else would he say?

The jury began deliberations last Friday and had not yet returned a verdict on Monday, December 15th.

County Bans Screaming Orgasm, Vets Screwed

About twice a year, a good old boy named J.O. Batten runs an "Old School Biker Rodeo Party in the Pasture" in his own private pasture in Hernando County, Florida.

Batten is about as good natured as a man can be. He put up with Paris Hilton and Nicole Ritchie living with him in 2004 for the second season of the "reality" television show *The Simple Life*. When he was younger, Batten also put up with a tour of duty in the Marine Corps in Vietnam.

Most of the proceeds from his "Party in the Pasture" go to a foundation that Batten and two other good Americans have started. It is called the DD-214 Foundation and Batten's partners in this endeavor are "DonV" Varrieur, who publishes a little magazine named *Scootergoods*, and a gentleman named "Chickenman" Morrison. If you do not know what a DD-214 is you probably don't need to know. It is not important. It is just a veteran's thing.

The last time Batten held his rodeo he hosted 2,200 guests and the next week he donated the profits, $11,000, to the Marine Corps League. The money went to veterans who were disabled or who were otherwise in distress.

Six months before that, the DD-214 Foundation donated another $10,069 in profits from the party in J.O.'s pasture. That money bought gasoline and airline tickets for visits from veteran's families, bought food for veterans and paid veteran's utility bills.

It is just a simple charity. The beneficiaries of these grants are screened by the James A. Haley Veterans Hospital in Tampa and the Hernando County, Florida office of the Veterans Administration.

Well, actually, it is a little more than only a charity. Just about everybody who has ever attended one of these parties has had a good time. These events hearken back to an earlier, simpler time; a time when it was a lot less work and a lot more fun to be a damn outlaw.

The beer at these things is cheap. The tee shirts are inexpensive. There are stupid bike games and burnouts and lots of women who are just a little bit on the trashy side. It is an adults only event.

It is not an event for the kind of people who run every local government in America. Anyone who has ever watched a local government govern, either in person or on public access television, knows what a local government is.

Local government is the same pathetic people who ran your Junior High student council, wasting two or three perfectly pleasant evenings a week making really boring, irrelevant and barely intelligible speeches at each other. Talk, talk, talk, talk, talk. Then, from time to time, they pass a law that the police then get to make all the rest of us obey.

Now, whether this is or this is not what Thomas Jefferson had in mind when he wrote his declaration is not what you need to know here.

All you need to know is that local government finally found out what the bikers in J.O. Batten's pasture have been up to the last couple of years. Somebody told them it was about "beer, tits and biker shenanigans." Oh no!

And then, as if that wasn't bad enough, they found out about the "screaming orgasm contest." Somebody put a 27 second video of one of the contestants up on You Tube. And, the Hernando County local government found it.

This video features an attractive, young woman with waist-long, blonde hair. She is wearing a pair of cutoff jeans and a tube top and she is vigorously humping all inhibition out of some sort of a saddle. It might be a motorcycle saddle. She raises a microphone to her mouth and screams in self-deprecating, mock passion.

Someone off camera says something like, "Baby, it don't normally happen that fast."

But, the attractive, young blonde ignores him. She rises, reverses her position and proceeds to once again make whatever the hell it is that she is humping the happiest whatever it is in the Sunshine State. One cannot help but conclude that if this blonde really likes a guy and he buys her dinner, then afterward, for dessert, he is probably going to have a real good night.

"Whoa!" Hernando County Commissioner Diane Rowden told the St. Petersburg *Times* about the video. "Um, I'm breathless," Rowden added cryptically. "This is a first."

It is impossible to tell from the *Times* account whether Ms. Rowden is actually outraged or whether she has just then decided that she needs to make some changes in her life —that she has to stop attending these stupid, local government meetings and instead go find herself a man that owns a leather jacket and join all of us on the dark side. Open minded, good hearted men might be inclined to think that even if she is now outraged all Ms. Rowden needs to change her mind is a good, long, hard motorcycle ride.

However there is no mistaking the County Commission's intent to run Batten and his DD-214 Foundation out of business. In 2002, Hernando County banned public nudity, and the county attorney has gone on record as saying Batten's party violates that ban, even if it is held in Batten's own private pasture, because the adult general public is invited and if you want to get in you have to pay $10.

This week, the county is threatening Batten with a $15,000 fine if he goes ahead with the party he has scheduled for this Halloween weekend.

And, Batten has appealed. He is scheduled to appear before the Commissioners tomorrow, September 23.

Methland

I was young. I was getting drunk in a dive in old Baja Oklahoma. It was so long ago the jukebox was wailing "Mendocino." It was so long ago the dancers all wore tassels and thongs. A strobe light throbbed like the end of sex so even if you stared you could only see about half of what all was going on.

Big Betty danced on a tiny stage across from the bar. Big Betty's best dance was when her feet stayed still. She leaned forward, put her hands on her knees and made her big, world famous breasts spin circles in opposite directions just like the rotors on a Chinook helicopter. Every strobe flash was a snapshot. Between flashes, the light behind the bar made her silver tassels blur. Big Betty would lean right over her audience and the audience would lean back so close that if they opened their mouths they could taste Big Betty's sweat.

One romantic offered Big Betty a drink from his bottle of beer. She took the bottle from his hand. Then disdaining a drink, just as she straightened to step back and dance with her feet again, Big Betty broke that bottle right across that romantic's head. The romantic staggered back heartbroken but he did not fall. Somebody caught him and pushed him toward the front door. He stumbled out blinded by his own blood.

He left a trail to follow but no one bothered. Some other dance aficionado stole that romantic's space near the edge of the stage. Throughout the night, boots and work shoes ground the pieces of that bottle back down to sand.

A Kiowa named Lynn danced for me, just for me, that night on my table while I pretended not to give a damn. I had been subtly admiring Lynn the Kiowa for at least weeks. She was little, beautiful and brown. When she shook her head in the flashing light her hair would explode like a startled murder of crows. Then it would all magically fall back to exactly the way it had been. Even in her stripper shoes she couldn't have been much more than five-foot-two. I don't know, maybe she was eighteen. She leered at me while she danced. She was flexible as a gymnast. She bent all the way over from the waist and put her face a foot from mine. She looked right through my eyes down to the Faustian depths of my soul. She wore that wanton look a woman wears when she tells you, "You can do anything you want."

And, she asked me, "Do you have any crystal meth?"

That was the very first time I ever heard it called that. Now, I have heard it called speed, ice, amp, glass, new school, crunch, whizz, fatch, rocket fuel and of course crank; because in the old days men used to smuggle it in motorcycle crankcases. I know at least a dozen more names. Bikers have names for methamphetamine like Eskimos have names for snow. There are different names when it is almost clear, pale yellow, tinged with violet or when it is brown and crunchy like peanut butter.

And, what I saw that night makes more sense when you understand that Big Betty and Lynn and some fraction of the rest of the people there that night were making the most of their lives through the magic of meth.

Psychoactive drugs resemble chemicals for which evolution has already reserved a place, or receptor, in the human brain. Amphetamines resemble adrenaline. They were isolated in Japan and issued to Japanese soldiers during the Russo-Japanese War. Twenty-five years later a Philadelphia pharmaceutical firm named Smith, Kline and French (SKF) pirated the Japanese research, patented the chemicals and started marketing a Benzedrine inhaler "for quick relief of cold symptoms." College students discovered what else amphetamines could do and in the late 30s SKF started marketing benzedrine as a treatment for fatigue, narcolepsy and obesity. During World War II SKF sold 180 million Benzedrine tablets to the U.S. Army and the tablets were also routinely fed to American troops in Korea and Vietnam.

Benzedrine is the most common brand name for the molecule 1-phenyl-2-aminopropane. A molecule with the same atomic components that assembles those atoms a little differently is brand named Dexedrine. If you methylate the final nitrogen atom in Dexedrine you make a molecule that was originally branded as Methedrine. The methylation makes methamphetamine harder to metabolize than Dexedrine, which means that meth has a longer half-life, which means it provides a longer, fuller, more satisfying high.

After SKF's patents expired in 1949 there was an explosion of amphetamine production and use. A scholar named David Courtwright called post-war America an "amphetamine democracy" because truck drivers, factory workers, students, housewives, politicians and celebrities all took amphetamines to help them lead better and more productive lives.

A New York society doctor named Max Jacobson got rich selling Dexedrine and

14

methamphetamine to celebrities. His clients included Johnny Mathis, Yul Brenner, Truman Capote, Cecil B. DeMille, Eddie Fisher, Otto Preminger, Anthony Quinn, Tennessee Williams and dozens of politicians including John F. Kennedy. Jacobson injected Jack Kennedy with either Methedrine or Dexedrine before at least two of Kennedy's debates with Richard Nixon in 1960. So while the very straight Nixon was obviously nervous and tentative under the hot lights in front of the television cameras Kennedy was focused, collected and supremely confidant.

American mommies got so hooked on amphetamine diet pills that early in 1973 the Bureau of Narcotics and Dangerous Drugs and the Food and Drug Administration began tighter regulation of the drugs. Coincidentally, around the same time, Smith Kline and French discovered a new disease among children. SKF found a surprisingly large number of American children suffered from a "complex and little-understood learning and behavior disorder called," at first, "minimal brain dysfunction."

The disease quickly became known as Attention Deficit Disorder. SKF scientists found that 69 percent of all hyperkinetic children who were fed "moderate doses" of Benzedrine and Dexedrine "improved." A very important man named Dr. Leon Eisenberg, Chief of Psychiatric Services at Massachusetts General Hospital, was trotted out to testify to the press that there was "no indication of addiction or other drug induced emotional or psychological damage" found in hyperactive children treated with amphetamine.

Amphetamines were marketed as "the penicillin of children with learning disabilities." An amphetamine named methylphenidate was branded as "Ritalin" and the healing began.

In the 70s cocaine, (a brand name coined by the Bayer Drug Company the same year Bayer coined the brand names Aspirin and Heroin) replaced amphetamines as a cure for celebrities' insecurity and housewives' chubbiness. But bennies, dex and meth remained firmly entrenched in the aspirations of the white working class. For decades in America, upward mobility and prosperity were connected, rightly or wrongly, with working longer and harder. Truck drivers, for example, were paid by the load. A trucker who drove 20 hours a day could make more money than one who only drove ten hours.

Piece work on a punch press machine is really only possible with the aid of some amphetamine. Grab a piece of metal from a box on your right, slip it into one of three dies, tap your right foot, flip the partially finished part into a second die, tap, slide it into a third die with your left hand, tap, toss the finished, or partially finished, piece into a box on your left and repeat 6,000 times. Don't screw up. You might lose a hand. Concentrate. Concentrate. Go home. Live your real life. Try to sleep. Get up. Repeat.

Or take the truck batteries off the pallet one by one and set them on the roller line. Drag the empty pallet to the other end of the line and restack the finished batteries. And, repeat, repeat, repeat, repeat, repeat. Don't think.

Or, the pre-eminent blue collar job, the job you had to know somebody to get. Scamper in front of a slowly moving line of cars and bolt on 52, or 56, or 61 bumpers an hour depending on how fast somebody a thousand miles away has decided the line must move that day. Do it hour after hour, day after day. Ask for overtime.

That was the seventies and the eighties. Those were the good, old days. Those were the jobs you could get before America became a "knowledge worker economy" and all the good, blue collar were assigned to slaves in China who live in dormitories.

After the jobs went away only the crank remained. Only the feeling of self-confidence and power methamphetamine promotes remained. And that is where Nick Reding picks up the story in his book *Methland: The Death and Life of an American Small Town*.

After methamphetamine use was increasingly criminalized in the early 1970s, after the flow of amphetamine from Mexico was interrupted, after the introduction of Sudafed made it comparatively easy to cook crank at home, after cocaine made powders chic, after freebase and crack, crank became a part of post-industrial American life. Crank became a get rich quick scheme. Crank became a cheap high. The line between buyers and sellers blurred. Motorcycle clubs in California and New Jersey competed for market share. The lingering effects of that competition persist today. Within the last five years even the New York Times and Newsweek have heard of crank.

Reding's book is full of defects and it is still the best thing yet written on the subject because Nick Reding may be the first insider writer to actually notice the connection between methamphetamine abuse and the shattering of the American dream. Reding started looking at Oelwein, Iowa (it is pronounced Ol' Wine) in 2005. Oelwein has a population of about 6,000 and before its disillusionment it was a quintessential American town. Most of Reding's book is a sympathetic portrait of the people he met there.

Reding, who knows nothing about motorcycle clubs, still tries to be kind to a Sons of Silence patch holder named "Major." Major worries about what his crank abuse might do or have done to his toddler son.

Reding tries to meet the county prosecutor, a man named Nathan Lein, halfway. The leading physician in Oelwein is a chain-smoking alcoholic named Clay Hallberg. A man named Roland Jarvis is such a grotesquely depraved crank fiend that the government should pay him to appear in anti-drug public service announcements.

The local Police Chief is a nut case named Jeremy Logan who intends to save Oelwein by telling his cops to "Assume everyone is guilty, and put the screws to them."

Reding's best source is a 45-year-old federal prisoner named Lori Arnold. Lori was born in the nearby town of Ottumwa and she is the sister of the character actor and comedian Tom Arnold.

Lori Arnold started selling pharmaceutical grade methamphetamine in the 1970s and she is the former wife of a man named Floyd Stockdall. Stockdall was a former President of the Grim Reapers Motorcycle Club, from whom the Sons of Anarchy have borrowed their patch.

And the Grim Reapers, according to Reding, had a connection to a fairly well known meth lab in Southern California back in the 80s. Lori tried crystal, liked it, and gave some away to her friends. Her friends liked crank, too and within a month Lori was buying four ounces of meth in Long Beach for $2,500 and selling it for $10,000 in Iowa. Her business grew from there and by 1987 Lori, who dropped out of school in the 10th grade, owned a bar, a car dealership, 14 houses, 52 racehorses and a 144 acre horse farm. That was the same year most of the other farms in that part of Iowa were foreclosed and most of the railroad and meatpacking jobs disappeared.

Lori Arnold was an inspiration to her neighbors. But she liked her own product too much to get out. The feds caught her in 1990 and she wound up doing nine years.

By the time Lori Arnold got out of prison in 1999 most of the straight jobs had disappeared, the average wage had dropped to five dollars an hour and

80 percent of the jobs still left were held by undocumented Mexican immigrants. She went to work for Cargill, slicing up hogs in a room so cold she had to pour hot water over her rubber boots to keep her feet from going numb. And, since she was bright and desperate, Lori Arnold couldn't help but notice that there was a racial divide between the high quality crank the Mexican workers used and the kitchen crank the white locals used. So like all good workers in the new knowledge worker economy, Lori Arnold used her mind.

By 2001, two years after she was sprung, Lori was selling so much Mexican crank to poor Iowa whites that she had to open another nightclub to launder all the money. Her success did not last long. On October 25th of that year she sold four ounces of meth to a local Iowa cop and returned to the penitentiary.

Since Methland was published last summer the reviews have been very mixed. Most of the critical reviews have scolded Reding for trying to do what this review has tried to do, which is to try to hint at "a unified theory of 'the meaning of meth.'"

Scott Martelle for example, a journalism instructor at Chapman University who wrote the review for the Los Angeles *Times*, cannot bring himself to believe that methamphetamine abuse might be in any way connected to the shattering of the American dream. Martelle writes: "At first, Reding argues, meth was viewed as a crutch by local workers looking for a little boost to get through long double shifts. It's not a persuasive argument. Substance abuse – from alcohol to pot to coke and now meth – in rural America has a lot of contributing factors, but the drive to work harder doesn't seem likely to rank high among them."

I think Reding's argument is persuasive and I think it is about time somebody who can actually get a book published said it. Nick Reding has gone and looked and tried to sympathize so he understands that crank abuse is not the disease. Crank abuse, like Gin abuse in Dickens' London, is a symptom of a disease that most cops, lawyers, judges, politicians, authors and, apparently, journalism instructors refuse to see. Reding sees what I see and so I think *Methland* deserves to be read.

Framing Dave Burgess

If you are reading this now you probably already know all about Dave Burgess. You know about his arrest and his conviction and you know about the stain that he must now wear for the rest of his life like a scarlet letter.

Most of what you think you know about Burgess is the work of a very competent, 31-year-old reporter named Matt Joyce. Joyce works for *The Associated Press* in Wyoming and whether you did or did not see his name at the top of your page, whether your anchor person mentioned him or not, Joyce was the guy who told you about the case.

Joyce deserves his job. He earned his Bachelor's Degree from Colorado College in Colorado Springs –a very expensive, liberal arts college for, mostly, the children of America's ruling class. He holds a Masters from the University of Texas at Austin. And besides the AP Joyce has worked for the Durango *Herald* and the Waco *Tribune-Herald*.

But, it is also fair to assume from his work that Joyce does not fear, hate or even distrust the police. Probably, he has never been "subdued" or lectured about life by a little, fat man in a judge dress. Nor is Joyce a member of what was once called the "working

21

press." Joyce belongs to what is now generally regarded to be the "professional press."

So Matt Joyce accurately reported what he saw and heard, he got some quotes and he moved on. He self-evidently never bothered to give Burgess' indictment and trial the thought it deserved. And, that is at least unfortunate.

Because a broader, less hurried and slightly more skeptical approach than Joyce took to the matter of the *United States of America, Plaintiff, v. David Burgess, Defendant, No. 07-CR-298-J* raises vexing issues about the policing of America in the new millennium.

In fact, the longer you stare at the case the more it starts to look like Dave Burgess might have actually been framed.

Burgess makes a good villain because he is an interesting man. And, as there is a Chinese curse, "May you live in interesting times," so there may be a way to curse a boy: "May you grow up to be an interesting man."

Even his enemies concede he has a few redeeming qualities. Burgess is artistically inclined. He likes to take photographs and he has posted many of them to a web site called *DavesWorld81*. Here and there among the snapshots are some real photographs. They are indistinguishable from the little frozen moments that hang on gallery walls on La Brea and in Chelsea. But, Burgess never tried to sell them. He just basically gave away what he saw to anybody who wanted to look.

He didn't have to sell his photographs, anyway. He usually had money, cars, motorcycles and a home. He married a knockout blonde. She was a former Budweiser girl and after they separated they remained business partners. Some men dream of harems. Burgess owned a whorehouse called the Old Bridge Ranch. And, in a year when Harley-Davidson is promising a guaranteed dose of outlaw mystique with the purchase of each and every 883cc Sportster, Dave Burgess was the President of the Nevada Nomads charter of the Hells Angels Motorcycle Club.

Burgess now may be one of the four Angels' patch holders every citizen knows: Sonny Barger, George Christie, Chuck Zito and Burgess. Whether you like him now or not, many men regard Burgess fondly. Ironically, many people find his sentimentality toward children to be his most appealing quality.

But, he could have been wiser. For example, he still calls himself "The Alpha Male," which begins to hint at the extent to which he miscalculated his life. Everybody who takes a moment to think knows that Dick Cheney is the new American Alpha Male.

Consequently, while Dick Cheney negotiates the price of his memoir Dave Burgess sits in the United States Penitentiary at Lompoc. The man who likes to see what other men cannot is currently trapped in a grey, concrete box surrounded by the exquisite California coast.

His release date is May 7th, 2021. If authorities think he becomes sufficiently rehabilitated he will be eligible for parole in 2013. If he is paroled on the earliest possible date he must still submit to the nagging indignity of supervision by a parole officer until 2023.

And, he must register as a sex offender for the rest of his life because last July he was convicted of the federal offense of possession and interstate transportation of child pornography.

It started on a lonely road in Wyoming.

US 80 is one of four Interstate Highways along with the 10, 40 and the 90, to which the 80 is sometimes joined, that traverse the entire breadth of the contiguous states. Burgess and another Hells Angel named Shayne Waldron got on the 80 in Reno and by ten o'clock in the morning on July 24, 2007 they had

23

gotten as far as Uinta County in the southwest corner of Wyoming.

Uinta County is cattle country. It holds fewer than 20,000 people. And, by the time you get there Route 80 has become a monotonous, four lane, split grey ribbon. It is surrounded by low, tan prairie at the Utah state line but soon climbs into a confusion of rocky hills.

The men were travelling in Burgess' white, Freight Liner motor home. Waldron was driving. The men were going to a Hells Angels national run in Eureka Springs, Arkansas and they were towing their bikes in a trailer. Looking out the window Burgess would have seen the original, transcontinental railroad line playing hide and seek with the modern interstate.

That section of road is regularly patrolled by a career, Wyoming Highway Patrol officer named Matthew Arnell. Arnell is a thick, jowly Navy veteran who is entering early middle age. He takes himself and his work seriously. He is on the Board of Directors of the Wyoming Highway Patrol Association. And, he had been "told at a briefing" to be on the lookout for Burgess, to stop him and to try to get something on him.

Arnell found Burgess and Waldron eating breakfast at a restaurant in Evanston, Wyoming. As the men ate, the Trooper found something in the parking lot. The bike trailer had an expired license plate. Arnell, as a legal tactic, waited for the two Angels to finish breakfast and leave. Then as he pulled out after them onto the interstate he called for a drug-sniffing dog.

He stopped the two for the expired trailer tag. The men explained, yeah, they knew and they told him they were on their way to Wamsutter, Wyoming, which would have been an hour and half away, to pick up another set of plates from the trailer's owner.

If the stop had been was the routine transaction it was later presented to be, Arnell would have written Burgess a ticket and let the men proceed. But it wasn't a routine stop. It was an entrapment so Arnell investigated while he waited for the drug sniffing dog to arrive. He inspected the interior of the trailer. He wrote down that the two men called each other brother. He attempted to verify what he already knew – that they were Hells Angels. He would later report that only after determining that the men were Hells Angels and smelling "the odor of burned marijuana" did he request the dog.

Smell is one of the most subjective senses but what is undeniable is that the there was no marijuana burning in the motor home at the time of the stop and neither Burgess nor Waldron were stoned. The subject of driving under the influence never even came up. The accusation was completely contrived.

Uinta County, Wyoming drug searches multiple times a day. The small, mostly rural county in the middle of cattle country has only two "Range Detectives" but it has three K9 units. Eventually, a thick man in blue jeans and a tan shirt arrived with a happy, slightly goofy Labrador retriever.

Arnell, it has always been obvious, was only looking for an excuse to toss the motor home. He was also thoroughly aware that he could not have searched the vehicle when it was still parked in the restaurant lot because legally, when parked, a motor home is a residence. He waited for the two men to start moving because then the motor home became a vehicle and the rules for searching a vehicle are much less strict than those that secure the privacy of a home.

Still, the cop tried to get consent to search. He said something like "There are no illegal drugs, atomic bombs, biological weapons, gold from Fort Knox, anything like that in there is there, gentlemen. Nothing in there you don't want me to know about, is there? Then you won't mind if I search the vehicle."

At the time of the traffic stop Burgess had a clean criminal record. He had been convicted of selling marijuana in the 1980s but the conviction had been overturned on appeal. Federal and local police in northern Nevada have publically acknowledged that they tried to "get" Burgess for years. So Burgess refused to consent to a search.

Eventually the handler compelled the Labrador to alert. The dog alerted on the state of Wyoming. The dog was outside the Freight Liner, on the driver's side and he smelled "something."

That alert led the K9 officer to lead the Lab around to the home's door and in its enthusiasm, as is the way with Labradors, the dog ran inside. Both Arnell and the dog handler observed that the Labrador looked "confused" and interpreted the dog's confusion as evidence that the dog was attempting to alert on "multiple locations" where drugs could be found.

The two cops then believed they had probable cause to search the motor home without a warrant. The point, actually, was to at least give a couple of Hells Angels a hard time and gather "gang intelligence." It was a very thorough roadside search.

The Freight Liner had two rooms and in the back room, the bedroom, Trooper Arnell found a K-Mart shopping bag with a small wood pipe inside. The story, the legal fiction, goes that Arnell thought the pipe "smelled like" marijuana and he then observed what he thought were "traces" of marijuana in the bag.

He searched all the clothing in the motor home and found nothing which he later said aroused his suspicion so he searched all the clothing again. This time Trooper Arnell found a piece of "tissue paper" inside a shirt. After searching the tissue paper he found what appeared to be a small amount of cocaine.

26

The drugs probably were not planted. Arnell, like other policemen, may carry small amounts of cocaine around with him to plant on deserving suspects but he probably did not do it this time. Unless Wyoming really intended to prosecute the two men for possession of small amounts of recreational drugs, all Arnell had to do was say he found the drugs, anyway. All that is necessary legally, to effect a search is to find "felony amounts" of an illegal drug and the whole point of the detention was to comb the motor home

Burgess admitted that the pipe in the plastic bag was his but the stop was never about drugs. The drug charge was a sham and was eventually dropped. Although Arnell never mentioned it in his affidavit he would have seen a Compaq laptop computer and a palm sized, Seagate, portable hard drive sitting in the bedroom. The most likely reason for the stop and fabricating a drug charge was to create a situation where national police forces including the ATF and the FBI could gather "gang intelligence." The whole point of seizing and searching the motor home would have been to seize and search the computers. Burgess and Waldron were both Mirandized, taken into custody and the home on wheels, the bike trailer and the bikes were all towed to a Wyoming Highway Department garage in Evanston.

Evanston is a nice, little city with a great view of the mountains for which Uinta County is named. It looks like the town in the movie Shane, only 140 years farther on in the history of the Republic. In Evanston, Arnell was met by a local Agent of the Wyoming Division of Criminal Investigation (DCI), named Russell Schmitt.

Schmitt tested the "white powder" Arnell "found" in the motor home. It tested positive as cocaine and at that moment, Russell Schmitt became the lead investigator in the case. Schmitt actually wrote the affidavit and went with Arnell to obtain a search warrant for the Freightliner. All of what Arnell and the dog handler had supposedly, previously done and said and observed were all actually written down by Schmitt. It is necessary to use the qualifier "supposedly" because Schmitt has a history with affidavits and search warrants.

Schmitt began his law enforcement career in a little department in Green River, Wyoming and while employed there he appeared in the middle of a case any Wyoming lawyer should know. Schmitt seems to have bullied and lied his way into effecting the arrest of a Green River "drug dealer" named Richard D. Cordova. Cordova was not exactly an outlaw and his naivety about police would later hinder his defense. Cordova basically threw himself on the mercy of the cops and wound up doing a couple of years in a penitentiary as a result.

The affidavit Schmitt wrote to get a search warrant in the Cordova case was questionable enough to eventually be reviewed by the Wyoming Supreme Court. "We agree that the affidavit in question comes uncomfortably close to violating the protections guaranteed Wyoming citizens," the court wrote about the pretense Schmitt had used to get the warrant. But "in deference to the judicial issuing officer," which is to say the judge Schmitt talked into issuing the warrant, Wyoming let Cordova's conviction stand.

In the end, the legal razor's edge that cut Cordova but not Schmitt was the fine line of "intent" – which may be even more subjective than the sense of smell. Cordova could not prove that Schmitt intentionally tried to violate the Constitutions of Wyoming and the United States. The Wyoming Supreme Court ruled that even if Schmitt had lied he had not lied "deliberately" and if he disregarded the truth he did not do so "recklessly."

So a cynic might conclude that Schmitt knew how to lie his way into a search of almost anything. It is virtually certain that Arnell and Schmitt had already booted up the computers and looked around before they ever applied for the warrant.

Schmitt carefully worded the affidavit and later, obviously, perjured himself in an evidence hearing by stating that it was perfectly normal and reasonable to search through all the records on somebody's personal computer if you could just catch them with personal use amounts of common recreational drugs.

"Based upon training and experience, your Affiant knows that persons involved in trafficking or the use of narcotics and dangerous drugs often keep photographs of coconspirators or photographs of illegal narcotics in their vehicle," Schmitt claimed. "Your Affiant knows that paraphernalia for packaging, cutting, weighing, and using is commonly kept in the vehicle of the drug trafficker. Subjects involved often keep pay-owe sheets, and receipts of customers and subjects also involved with drug trafficking keep weapons to protect there (sic) Narcotics and drug proceeds."

This was two guys on vacation in an off-brand Winnebago.

The last three Presidents have all admitted to using marijuana, although Clinton preposterously claimed to have never "inhaled." George W. Bush is, reportedly, a recovering cocaine fiend. So, does that mean that if George W. Bush is travelling through Wyoming one day and Russ Schmitt catches him with one of his old marijuana pipes that Schmitt can then go through all of Bush's computer records? Because Bush might be a drug dealer? Because he probably stores his drug dealer's scrap book on his PC?

Who believes that? A Circuit Court Judge named Michael Greer believes that. He issued the warrant.

Decide for yourself if Schmitt perjured himself or not. This is from a transcript of an evidentiary hearing.

Question: And why did you think that it was important to take that computer and that hard drive that you saw right there?

Agent Schmitt: Well, 'cause, you know, we'd already found cocaine and marijuana, and, you know, there's a good chance that, one, it would have pictures of coconspirators or other people or e-mails of drug trafficking or the person that drove the vehicle itself standing there with drugs to show that, yes, this person is into drugs or, I mean, several reasons.

Question: So photographs certainly?

Agent Schmitt: Yes, sir.

Question: Names or information pertaining to other people that might be engaged in illegal activity?

Agent Schmitt: E-mails.

Question: E-mails that might show or relate to illegal activity relating to these controlled substances or controlled substances; is that correct?

Agent Schmitt: Yes. In a lot of them we've confiscated several computers where they are actually downloading things on how to make methamphetamine, recipes. And I think that—to be honest, I believe that's—I know there wasn't methamphetamine found at this, but that kind of started the trend for taking computers 2 years ago because of the downloading of methamphetamine recipes, and then it just kind of went from there to be more mainstay all the time.

Schmitt and Trooper Arnell tossed Burgess' motor home a second time. We are to believe, everyone is supposed to believe, that Trooper Arnell's roadside search, when he unfolded all of Burgess' and Waldron's shirts twice and went through their socks and their underwear was a "cursory search." And, the reason we should believe this is because we are also supposed to believe that Arnell never saw the computer and the portable hard drive just sitting there. We are to believe that the two men did not discover the computer equipment until the second search.

During this second, more thorough search at the Evanston garage, and aided by his ghost writer Agent Schmitt, Trooper Arnell "discovered" a second, palm-sized, portable hard drive. Arnell found a Maxtor drive "under one of the couches in the motor home, when he slipped his hand into a very small opening under the seat of the couch and had to remove his wristwatch to get his hand back out of that opening."

No other drugs or evidence of drug dealing or drug manufacture were found. No other contraband was found: No guns, switchblade knives, samurai swords, atomic bombs, biological weapons or large amounts of cash, that sort of thing.

Thorough professionals that they are, Arnell and Schmitt then stepped away from the case and went to do more important police work –keeping gangs, for example, from moving into Wyoming from urban areas like Utah. Schmitt turned the computer equipment over to a Wyoming DCI Intelligence Analyst named Elvin Ehrhardt on July 25th, the day after the traffic stop.

And, the fact that the hardware was turned over to Agent Ehrhardt is interesting because it demonstrates where the state of Wyoming, and particularly the Federal Bureau of Investigation (FBI), were going with the case. Ehrhardt is the Wyoming DCI "authority" on street gangs. It was his job to gather and interpret "intelligence" about motorcycle clubs.

Agent Ehrhardt took the computer and drives to the offices of the Wyoming Internet Crimes Against Children (ICAC) Team. The ICAC comprises five DCI agents, one Immigration and Customs Enforcement

(ICE) agent and one agent from the FBI. Even presuming that the U.S. Department of Justice did not know they had Burgess by the short hairs before, the FBI knew after that. And, where they stored Burgess hardware was in an office full of child pornography.

Since Ehrhardt is a "gang expert," and most law enforcement agencies consider the Hells Angels to be a "gang" you might expect him to retain custody of this "evidence." But, Ehrhardt transferred custody of the hardware to another DCI cop, Special Agent Randall Huff.

Huff is a very experienced and computer savvy cop. He served as a uniformed officer for six years. He has worked for the Division of Criminal Investigation since 1990 and he has worked as a trainer for other departments throughout the United States on how to seize and exploit computer evidence. Most of his work involves child pornography. Huff's work does not involve, as Agent Schmidt put it, "…computers where they are actually downloading things on how to make methamphetamine, recipes. And I think that—to be honest, I believe that's—I know there wasn't methamphetamine found at this, but that kind of started the trend for taking computers 2 years ago because of the downloading of methamphetamine recipes, and then it just kind of went from there to be more mainstay all the time."

Agent Huff held the hardware for a week, without looking at it – or so the story of the official chain of custody of the evidence goes. Then he gave the hardware to yet another DCI cop, Special Agent Scott Hughes. And, then Agent Hughes finally began his "preliminary forensic examination" of the laptop and the two hard drives.

Then Hughes paused for 20 days. Maybe the ICAC is a no-smoking office. The official explanation is that he was waiting for a copy of Judge Greer's Search

Warrant. The warrant finally arrived on August 21. And, immediately Agent Hughes had a meeting with the Senior Assistant Attorney General of the State of Wyoming, David L. Delicath. Not a staff attorney. The Senior Assistant Attorney General.

David Burgess' computer hardware, the evidence that had been seized –rather than subpoenaed—because it might reveal fleeting intelligence about the identities of drug dealers or possibly a new recipe for crank was passed from cop to cop four times, stored in an office containing child pornography and at least one known FBI Agent, and then before anyone would examine it the Agent who had custody of it asked "the advice" of the Senior Assistant Attorney General of the State of Wyoming.

Purportedly, the conversation was about "the scope of the search warrant." But again, cynics who have actually been to court might be inclined to think that what was happening was all the cops were getting their stories together.

Finally, 16 days after that, Agent Hughes, according to public documents, finally "began the process of acquiring (or copying) and previewing the contents of the Maxtor External Hard Drive." The Maxtor was the hard drive Trooper Arnell found hidden in a couch. And, its discovery was so memorable that Arnell remembers he almost lost his watch. Which is an exquisite detail. It lends what writers call verisimilitude. It is a graphic detail that makes a story sound true.

There is a fairly standard protocol for the forensic examination of computer hardware called, "Forensic Examination of Digital Evidence: A Guide for Law Enforcement." It was published by the Department of Justice in 2004 and the deliberateness with which Agent Hughes conducted his examination seems to indicate he had a least heard of the document.

One of the key first steps in a computer forensic examination is to ensure that the hard disk is "write protected." Agent Hughes, simply by reading the manual, would have known to do that, but there is no indication that any of Burgess' computer equipment was ever write protected before August, 1st.

The software Agent Hughes employed to search the Maxtor hard drive is a low end –about $700—but standard suite of evidence acquisition tools used in computer forensic examinations called "EnCase." Law enforcement agencies use EnCase because it is a most excellent tool for finding only what the search warrant says the cops are looking for. The EnCase developer brags:

"SMART EVIDENCE COLLECTION: no other forensic tool gives organizations the ability to forensically preserve only the relevant evidence without capturing the entire hard drive."

In Burgess's case Hughes, purportedly, would have been looking for "text strings," what geeks call words, like "crack," "crank," "HA" or maybe, "my new recipe for making methamphetamine."

Recreational drugs were still what the case was supposed to be about. Every cop connected to the case, including Agent Hughes, testified under penalty of perjury that from July 24th until September 6th the case against Dave Burgess was about suspicion of drug dealing. The putative reason for conducting a search of Burgess' hard drives was to find evidence of drug dealing. But Agent Hughes did not look for that.

It is a widely held belief that the sort of computer searches conducted on Dave Burgess' computer equipment are intended to "accidently discover" child pornography. Steve Kalar, the senior federal public defender in San Francisco, told the National Journal that federal investigators "routinely search seized computers for evidence of...child pornography" on

34

hard drives. "It's a technological fallacy to say that an agent is tripping through the computer and finds this," Kalar said.

That is exactly what Agent Hughes said he did.

According to public documents, Agent Hughes, 44 days after the traffic stop: "...on September 6, 2007, began the process of acquiring (or copying) and previewing the contents of the Maxtor External Hard Drive. The EnCase preview function utilized by Special Agent Hughes permitted him to view images while the process of acquiring the contents of the hard drive proceeded. This preview revealed 'multiple images of child exploitation.' Special Agent Hughes testified he noted the name of the file, minimized the image, allowed the acquisition process to continue, but immediately stopped looking at images. Thereafter, a search warrant was applied for and obtained in Laramie County, Wyoming, which authorized the search of the laptop and the two external hard drives. Following execution of the search warrants specific to the laptop and external hard drives, further evidence of child exploitation was found and the instant charges were brought against defendant Burgess."

The official version of Burgess' crime and punishment a highly trained policeman doing routine police work in a highly professional laboratory found prima facie evidence of a damning crime. Just like on CSI.

There are, however two exculpatory possibilities: The hardware seized from Burgess was altered; or, the hardware seized from Dave Burgess was replaced.

Everybody who does computer forensics understands that portable hard drives are used to archive data that was originally collected and assembled somewhere else. But no evidence of that collection and assembly of Burgess' alleged, mind-boggling collection of kiddie porn was ever found.

The police looked. The FBI looked. Agents assigned to the Reno Resident Agency of the Las Vegas Field Office of the FBI raided Burgess' home and seized every piece of computer equipment they could find. They also would have looked for photographs, books and magazines. But they never found how or where Burgess got all the pictures he was accused of possessing.

It was never offered as evidence but the FBI would have also tracked all of Burgess internet use for years and no evidence of the origin of all this pornography was ever found. The FBI, at least during the Bush Administration, would not even have needed a search warrant. Americans, particularly Americans who have somehow come to the attention of one of the federal police forces, are now the subjects of a distressing amount of "shared electronic surveillance." Most of this surveillance remains invisible because it is rarely used in a prosecution but it is gathered nevertheless. It even has a name: "Intelligence Driven Law Enforcement."

There is an "Intelligence Architecture Plan" with the goals of "deconfliction, pointer index, case support, target profiles, intelligence fusion, and predictive analysis." It is the domestic equivalent of the War on Terror "Fusion Centers" but the domestic intelligence plan does not even pretend to be about national security. It is entirely geared to spying on people like Dave Burgess. Still nobody ever determined where the pornography Burgess was accused of possessing originated.

It is more certain, because of traceable serial numbers, to determine where the Seagate and Maxtor hard drives seized from the Burgess' Freightliner were bought. Credit card records prove that Dave Burgess bought portable hard drives similar to those "recovered" from the motor home. He bought them in Reno, near where he lives. The drives Hughes examined were purchased in Las Vegas, at the opposite end of the state.

Supposedly, Burgess' computer hardware contained a carefully cataloged library of 60,000 images and the point of prosecuting people who possess these images is to protect the children in those pictures. It might be an inherently flawed strategy. It might be like prosecuting random crack addicts for running the Cali Cartel.

But whether it is a good law or not, a smart law or not, almost everybody who might read this will agree wholeheartedly and unreservedly that child pornography is wrong and should be stopped and the children who are exploited should be rescued.

So, the question might then be raised, how many children were rescued as a result of the photographs found on Burgess' hard drive? How many missing children were identified? How many children? Nobody would expect the Wyoming Internet Crimes Against Children Team, or the FBI, or the National Center for Missing and Exploited Children to identify any of these kids but where were they? When were they? Isn't that the point of this case?

Or, was the point of this case to link the text strings "Hells Angels" and "Kiddie Porn" together in a headline?

Before you make up your mind about Dave Burgess you should also know that the FBI has been trying to pin something on him for a very long time – maybe as far back as the mid-seventies.

Dave Burgess is the nephew of Joseph and Sally Conforte. Joe Conforte opened a legal brothel called the Mustang Ranch in 1971. In its heyday the Mustang was the third largest employer in Storey County,

Nevada – after a pet food factory and the school system – and the taxes it paid provided about an eighth of the County's budget.

The Mustang Ranch replaced the "Best Little Whorehouse in Texas" as the most famous brothel in the world. To the world outside Storey County, the place, in the words of one author, "represented 'badness' on multiple levels." Despite, or maybe because of, its "badness" the Mustang eventually became three whorehouses: Mustang One, Mustang Two and, about 150 yards away from those two buildings, the Old Bridge Ranch.

The Mustang was notorious for almost 20 years and Dave Burgess was managing the place shortly before it was eventually closed down by the Federal Government in 1990. Joe Conforte and a Storey County Commissioner named Shirley Colletti were indicted for fraud and racketeering and Conforte disappeared.

By the time his uncle escaped Dave Burgess had split off and was operating the Old Bridge as a separate business. That and the fact that he was his uncle's nephew and that he had managed the Mustang were probably enough to make him one of the FBIs "usual suspects."

All cops know that everybody breaks the law. Everybody. It can't be helped. There are so many laws. Most of the time cops just stare out at everybody until they see one of us breaking a law. Sometimes, if cops do not like your attitude, they will ignore everybody else and just stare at you.

Something like that happened to Dave Burgess. The cops paid extra special attention to the Old Bridge Ranch.

Federal prosecutors went after Burgess' in-laws. Burgess' father-in-law, Jay "Cowboy" Rigas and his son Troy were indicted for being the "drug kingpins" of

Northern Nevada. Both men worked at the Old Bridge Ranch, which they all seemed to consider as a "family business," and both were convicted after an almost year-long trial for selling cocaine.

It was a classic example of legal musical chairs. Twenty-four people were alleged to have sold cocaine in Nevada, Northern California and Washington. Twenty-two of them turned state's evidence, sat in witness chairs and testified that it was all Jay and Troy Rigas' idea. Jay and Troy were left standing when it came time for somebody to be sentenced. Jay Rigas is still in jail and many law-abiding people honestly think that his trial was a miscarriage of justice.

Dave Burgess' mother-in-law, Yvonne Rigas, was so incensed by what she considered to be the railroading of her husband and son that she passed out leaflets in the courthouse parking lot. The leaflets were the product of a Libertarian group in Montana called the "Fully Informed Jury Association." The papers said, "True Or False? When you sit on a jury, you have the right to vote your conscience."

So, after her husband and son were locked up Yvonne Rigas was indicted for conspiracy and jury tampering for putting the papers on the wind shields of cars. It was a blatantly bogus charge. And, it could also be interpreted to mean that the United States of America was conducting a vendetta against the family that still ran what was left of the Mustang.

The long history of the official harassment of Dave Burgess and his uncle and his in-laws could fill a book. Burgess had numerous tax audits and suits disputing whether whores are employees or independent contractors and whether Troy Rigas, who Burgess rehired after his release from prison, was a moral enough person to work in a whorehouse and so on.

39

It is a dreary litany. Washington and Jefferson might have found it sad. But then, what would Andrew Jackson have done to Trooper Arnell?

The more Burgess was legally harassed the more alienated from the legal process he seemed to become. It was particularly not helpful to his cause that he became a member of the Hells Angels. Troy Rigas and another brother named Sohn Rigas also became Hells Angels and Sohn Rigas was charged with racketeering for tackling a Mongol during the infamous brawl between the two clubs at Harrah's in Laughlin in 2002.

Most police agencies assume that the Hells Angels are a criminal organization. No one has ever proved that the Hells Angels are the Mafia but that is exactly who police think they are. So, as time went by and the files the FBI kept on Burgess grew, Dave Burgess started to look more and more like Michael Corleone.

Worst of all, the cops could never get Burgess. The closest they came was his conviction for "conspiring to possess marijuana" that was later overturned. It is easy to imagine the cops laughing bitterly. The real Michael Corleone! An innocent man! Hah!

Then, Burgess was riding as a passenger in a white motor home that was stopped for a routine traffic violation in Wyoming in late July, 2007. And, suddenly the guy who was so smart that law enforcement couldn't touch him was revealed to be a moron who was so stupid that he had never bothered to encrypt his giant collection of child pornography.

Or, maybe Dave Burgess was framed.

Maybe in the George W. Bush America, during the war on terror, during the Alberto Gonzales administration of the Department of Justice, after Tommy Chong, in an age when even the Girl Scouts can legally be categorized as a "street gang," maybe a "naive" person, maybe an idealist might think it is possible that Dave Burgess was framed.

And, all of this happened before the AP's man in Wyoming, Matt Joyce, ever heard Dave Burgess' name. Then the headlines started. "HELLS ANGELS! KID PORN!!"

Burgess' Reno home was invaded by a SWAT Team in October, the house was searched but no evidence of child pornography either in digital or printed form was found.

Burgess has stated that at the time of that raid he was told by FBI Agents, "…if I did not agree to get the Hells Angels Motorcycle Club involved in some criminal adventure they (the FBI) would make sure to make me look so bad that even my brothers in the Hells Angels would disown me, and that I would spend the next 20 years in prison branded as a pedophile!"

Burgess has also protested that the "…U.S. attorney offered me a deal, but part of the deal was that I would lose my brothel (not sell it, just close it and lose it.) Again, I said no deal."

Burgess was indicted on November 14. He appeared before a judge 12 days later and at that hearing the prosecutor, James C. Anderson, asked the magistrate to deny Burgess bail because he was a member of the Hells Angels. Burgess pleaded not guilty the next day and went on trial in April.

"Investigators found tens of thousands of child pornography images, carefully organized and explicitly labeled, on computer equipment belonging to Nevada brothel owner and Hells Angel member David Burgess," was how Matt Joyce led his story on Wednesday, April 16th.

America was further informed that Burgess' computer hardware "revealed just an almost unimaginable amount of child pornography" on those hard drives. "We're talking about crime scene photographs of young children being treated in a way that no child should be treated."

Burgess was represented by a Public defender named James H. Barrett. Burgess had a $2 million IRS lien against his personal assets at the time of his indictment. And, both Burgess and the prosecutor seemed to regard Barrett as a nitwit.

Barrett knew it, too. "The Defendant has indicated in open court that he lacks confidence in Counsel and has, as well...indicated the likelihood that he will seek to

question the effectiveness of counsel in the conduct of his defense," Barrett complained to the Judge in the last of his multiple attempts to withdraw from the case. The judge let Barrett resign after Burgess was convicted. Burgess' attorney at sentencing was Dion Custis, an attorney who had a brief moment of fame when he represented a defendant named Aaron McKinney who was convicted in a widely reported case of killing a homosexual college student named Matthew Shepard.

The child pornography actually entered into evidence against Burgess, and found on his hard drive, were a half dozen sexually provocative images of an adolescent girl Burgess actually knew. Burgess had a romantic relationship with the girl's mother and he has always maintained that he does not know how the images got there. The girl's mother testified at Burgess' trial that Burgess never had the opportunity to take the photos. Most people who know both Burgess and the girl believe the girl uploaded the images herself. Several of the photos had bawdy captions superimposed on them. The captions were made with a common piece of software called Adobe Photoshop. It is also a fact that Burgess never owned Photoshop and instead used an old copy of software called Corel Photo Paint for every caption and photo enhancement he is known to have ever made.

Burgess' defense was further hampered by a naivety about computers in general by the presiding judge, his defense attorney and probably the jurors. It seems to have never occurred to the defense attorney to hire his own computer expert.

Most of the testimony in the case was intended to establish that Burgess was a member of the Hells Angels who ran a whore house.

Troy Rigas and Burgess' estranged wife Ingrid both testified that Burgess. whether he was an outlaw or not, whether he used recreational drugs and ran a legal whorehouse or not, was not a man fixated on the sexualization of little children. Troy Rigas said the Hells Angels would not tolerate it. Ingrid Burgess testified that she had "known David for many years, almost 30 years. I've been around him a lot, and I know he wouldn't do anything like this."

The jury was unmoved. They believed the cops. They deliberated for less than four hours before they found Burgess guilty.

Burgess continued to protest his innocence and that annoyed the judge, an experienced and sometimes liberal jurist named Alan B. Johnson. "I would hope that at some point this defendant will be able to acknowledge his preoccupation with child pornography and the damage it has done to his life, his business and his family members," Johnson lectured Burgess.

Then Judge Johnson sentenced Burgess to 15 years in prison, ten years of supervision upon release, lifetime registration as a sex offender and a fine of $20,000.

Burgess replied, "The only thing that I have to say is I just apologize for having put the court through this."

Afterward, Judge Johnson dismissed the notion that Burgess might have been framed saying, "There is absolutely no evidence of that."

The next day, Matt Joyce reported, "A former Nevada brothel owner has been sentenced to 15 years in federal prison for his conviction on two child pornography charges in Wyoming." It was a simple and straightforward report and there followed a little storm of sensation. The suspicions and fears of a million people who have never actually met a Hells Angel were confirmed. The titillating sordidness of the American sex business was confirmed. The vigilance and righteousness of the police was confirmed. Faith in law and order was restored.

Outside of the Hells Angels, nobody thought Dave Burgess was framed.

Dave Burgess' Appeal

Dave Burgess continues to await the return of his good name and his freedom.

Burgess was the outspoken President of the Nevada Nomads charter of the Hells Angels Motorcycle Club and the proprietor of a legal whorehouse called the Old Bridge Ranch near Reno, Nevada. Burgess claimed for years that our government was out to get him. And, he was probably right.

Two years ago Burgess was the victim of a "routine traffic stop." Last summer, as a direct result of that stop, he was convicted of being so addicted to child pornography that he literally had to carry around with him "a catalogue" of 65,000 images of little children being raped. He was so addicted that he had to carry his "catalogue" across state lines. Even to Hells Angels national runs.

Burgess' trial was very widely publicized to illustrate the kind of perverts who are inclined to join motorcycle clubs in general and the Hells Angels in particular.

A federal judge in Cheyenne, Wyoming named Alan B. Johnson found Burgess guilty of an unacknowledged "addiction" to child pornography and sentenced him to 15 years in prison, ten years of supervision upon release, lifetime registration as a sex offender and a fine of $20,000. Burgess is currently locked up in the United States Penitentiary at Lompoc, California.

Last week, after a series of delays, the argument over Burgess' appeal was finally heard before a three-judge panel in Denver.

Burgess' 32 page appeal brief argues that his conviction should "be reversed because it was obtained in violation of his rights guaranteed by the Fourth Amendment and in violation of his right to a fair trial. Alternatively, his sentence must be vacated and the case remanded for resentencing."

The brief specifically argues that police, even in the cowboy states, cannot just take a computer from someone's motor home, keep it for months and then search it to see what might possibly be there to find. The brief argues that the police have a constitutional obligation to say what they are looking for and also accuses authorities of acting in bad faith.

Burgess' appeal also implies that the government was inventing its prosecution as it went along. One particularly damning invention was the insinuation before the jury that Burgess might have had or been contemplating an affair with a 13-year-old girl. All the government was trying to do, the brief argues, was put that idea in the jury's mind. And, Judge Johnson was wrong when he let the prosecution get away with that.

The brief concludes by arguing that even if Dave Burgess was guilty, he was still sentenced more harshly than he should have been because Johnson misinterpreted federal sentencing guidelines.

Burgess is represented in his appeal by Norman R. Mueller. Mueller is a highly regarded criminal appeals specialist who graduated from Yale Law in 1974.

Mueller's argument was heard by three experienced judges: Deanell Reece Tacha, Terrence L.

O'Brien and Michael W. McConnell. The three judges do not have to agree. The appeal may be accepted or denied by a vote of two to one.

With all due respect to the grand majesty and overall swellness of the Tenth Circuit Court of Appeals, Burgess seems, at first glance, to be outnumbered. All three of the judges who heard his case were appointed by law and order presidents. None of them seems to have ever been described as a civil libertarian.

Tacha is a handsome, grandmotherly woman who is usually photographed with a big grin on her face. She is a former law school professor who was appointed to the court by Ronald Reagan in 1985. Terrence L. O'Brien was appointed by George W. Bush in September, 2001 but was not confirmed for four months which indicates that he might have been slightly too ideologically pure for some Democrats. The third, and possibly the most scholarly of the three jurists, is Michael W. McConnell. McConnell was also appointed by George W. Bush largely because of his moralizing and his opposition to abortion.

The argument for upholding Burgess' conviction was presented by James Anderson, the same United States Attorney who convicted Burgess in the first place.

The time between which the oral arguments in a federal appeal are heard and the date on which a decision is finally rendered is usually about four and a half months. It is not uncommon for the long pause between the last word of the last argument and the first word of the courts reply to stretch out as long as 12 months. The Seventh Circuit, which is the most punctual circuit, usually takes about 3 months to actually decide a case.

Burgess' fate may be decided by the Fourth of July but the court will probably wait until Labor Day to publish its opinion.

Dave Burgess And BALCO

The computer forensics techniques that convicted former Nevada brothel owner Dave Burgess 14 months ago have been ruled unconstitutional in the Ninth Federal Judicial Circuit.

Those forensics remain technically legal in the Tenth Federal Judicial Circuit where Burgess' appeal was denied. But since federal law – theoretically, ideally, as it is described to little children – is supposed to be the same throughout the Federal Union, the legality of the forensics that convicted Burgess will have to be decided by the Supreme Court of the United States.

The Tenth Judicial Circuit includes Wyoming, Utah, Colorado, New Mexico, Kansas and Oklahoma. The Ninth Circuit rules on federal appeals originating in Washington, Oregon, Idaho, Montana, California, Nevada, Arizona, Alaska, Hawaii, Guam and the Marianas. Burgess lived in Nevada and is imprisoned in California but he was convicted in Wyoming and his appeal of that conviction was denied in Colorado.

Burgess is a former president of a charter of the Hells Angels Motorcycle Club. He owned a legal brothel in Nevada named the Old Bridge Ranch. He is the nephew of a man named Joseph Conforte who opened a very famous legal brothel called the Mustang

Ranch in 1971. Federal officials carried out a long, foul, moral war against everything and everyone connected to the Mustang Ranch starting in the Nixon Administration. Consequently, Burgess has suffered intermittent police harassment throughout most of his adult life.

Burgess was the target of a traffic stop in Wyoming in July 2007. The stop, as well as most of what followed, seems to have been cynically and meticulously game planned. After an extensive search of his motor home, that included multiple searches of the clothes in his closet, his wastebasket and his sock drawer, Burgess was charged with possession of small amounts of cocaine and marijuana and a pipe police described as "drug paraphernalia." Those drug charges were later dropped.

The traffic stop and the drug charges were merely the means by which federal and Wyoming officials, including the Attorney General of Wyoming and the Federal Bureau of Investigation, contrived a search of Burgess' laptop computer and two portable hard drives. A reasonable disagreement can be drawn as to whether the police knew what they were going to find before they looked or whether they were merely, innocently poking through Burgess' life to find whatever turned up.

The computer search revealed "images of child exploitation." Burgess was tried and convicted of knowingly transporting child pornography across state lines. He was sentenced to 15 years in prison, ten years of supervision upon release, lifetime registration as a sex offender and a fine of $20,000.

The Aging Rebel concluded some months ago that Dave Burgess was framed. It is now impossible for Burgess to prove his actual innocence. The issue upon which Burgess' freedom now rests is whether the search of his electronic equipment did or did not violate the Constitution of the United States.

Everyone who serves the United States, whether as a lowly private or as the President, vows to "preserve, protect and defend the Constitution of the United States." Fighting to preserve, protect and defend the fundamental law that ensures our freedom is how all those names got on that black wall.

The most fundamental of American laws states in part: "The right of the people to be secure in their persons, houses, papers, and effects, against unreasonable searches and seizures, shall not be violated, and no Warrants shall issue, but upon probable cause, supported by Oath or affirmation, and particularly describing the place to be searched, and the persons or things to be seized."

Over the last two centuries, the Constitution has been tortured by scholarly interpretation, politics and the police and several "exceptions" have been devised to what is usually called the "particularity requirement" in the passage quoted above.

Above all, a search must be "reasonable." One of elements of a reasonable search is that an impartial magistrate must first issue a warrant authorizing that search. And another element of a reasonable search is that the search warrant must particularly describe the place to be searched and the items to be seized.

An exception to the need for a warrant occurs when the place to be searched is highly mobile like an automobile. And, an exception to the "particularity requirement" occurs when a policeman sees evidence or contraband "in plain sight."

The problem with computer searches is that once you look into a hard drive, everything is in plain sight. And, as a general rule, this obvious fact never registered with any judge until two weeks ago. So, in a breathtakingly short span of years, computer searches

50

have become the preferred method used by career police and professional prosecutors to subvert the Constitution of the United States.

Today, at least 50 percent of all criminal cases in the United States rely on what law enforcement officials call "e-forensics" or electronic forensics. E-forensics includes the scientific examination of computers and portable computer media; the collecting and snooping-into of email; the monitoring and tracking of web browsing activity using IP addresses; the official and clandestine use of mal-ware; the cloning of and forensic examination of cell phones, cell phone SIMM cards, iPods and PDAs; the forensic examination of DVRs and GPS locators; the identification through code or so-called "fingerprinting" of both laser and ink jet computer printers and scanners; and the forensic examination of home computer routers and automobile black boxes.

Some of these techniques are bullet-proof. Some of them, like the techniques being investigated at Purdue University into the fingerprinting of inkjet printers, are very questionable. Police use all of these techniques every day. And, the manner in which all of these techniques are used to prosecute citizens hides in a Constitutional penumbra.

Twenty years ago if you had said "e-forensics" nobody would have known what you were talking about. Exactly as if you had said "iPod" 20 years ago people would have thought you were either a foreigner or just odd. Today, even stupid police are sophisticated about e-forensics. Today, even very bright defendants remain touchingly naïve about the trail of electronic bread crumbs they leave behind them everywhere they go. And, the naïveté of judges and defendants about e-forensics has given unscrupulous prosecutors an enormous advantage in the boardwalk game called criminal justice.

Intrinsic to the electronic creation and storage of data with all commercially available operating systems is the data's indiscretion. Computer cops commonly refer to this data as "ESI," or "electronically stored information."

The first step in entering ESI into evidence is to preserve it. What we are really talking about saving are electrons. And the reliability of this preservation is entirely dependent on a police officer who has a cynical interest in the case. His disinterest in the case is guaranteed by his "oath" as an officer of the court. And, whether he is good at his job or not he is always reckoned to be an "expert."

Current practice dictates that an e-forensics technician must preserve and examine all the contents of every device he examines. On a hard drive, the evidence the technician seeks might be scattered among several physical locations anywhere on the card, chip or drive. In the Burgess case, a hard drive was searched simultaneous to the preservation of its the contents. And, right there, in "plain sight" the technician would later testify, was a giant collection of child pornography.

The plain sight exception to computer searches makes every computer search a dragnet search. Everybody has known this for at least a couple of years except federal judges who, just like privates and presidents, must take an oath to preserve, protect and defend the Constitution. Just as John McCain famously did not understand how to send an email, federal judges are generally as ignorant about e-forensics as the "criminals" who stand trembling before them every day.

Dave Burgess got hit with a double whammy of Fourth Amendment exceptions. Because his motor home was moving police used the "automobile exception" to search his vehicle's contents, find the drugs he was taking with him on vacation and seize his computers and hard drives. Because he was holding recreational amounts of marijuana and cocaine and because he was a member of the Hells Angels Motorcycle Club he was "reasonably" assumed to be a drug kingpin.

Consequently, a local magistrate who could not tell the Constitution from a slice of Swiss cheese warranted the search of Burgess' laptop and drives under the pretense that they might "reasonably" be expected to hold "trophy photos" of him with great piles of narcotics, or "ledger sheets" of his imaginary drug business or "lists" of his imagined drug co-conspirators. What the police found, after 45 days of storing these electronics in a room filled with child pornography, was a huge collection of child pornography including indecent pictures of an adolescent girl Burgess actually knew.

Last May, Burgess appealed that conviction, in part, on the grounds that, "in this age of the laptop computer..." allowing overly broad searches "...would destroy a citizen's expectation of privacy in his or her computer."

"The modern development of the personal computer," the appeal continued, "and its ability to store and intermingle a huge array of one's personal papers in a single place increases law enforcement's ability to conduct a wide-ranging search into a person's private affairs."

But the Tenth Circuit Court of Appeals agreed with Boris Pasternak's Bolshevik fanatic Pasha in *Doctor Zhivago*. "Personal life," Pasha decreed, in case you have forgotten the book, "is dead."

The Tenth Circuit said it understood a laptop computer to be a kind of a "briefcase." If the Tenth Circuit's comparison was right, it would seem reasonable to then ask whether a searcher is entitled to read a suspect's diary just because it happens to be in that briefcase when what the searcher is supposed to be looking for is a gun. But the court snidely tossed that issue away. "One might speculate whether the Supreme Court would treat laptop computers, hard drives, flash drives or even cell phones as it has a briefcase or give those types of devices preferred status because of their unique ability to hold vast amounts of diverse personal information," the court wondered. Then added, "Interesting as the issue may be, we need not now resolve it...."

But just fifteen days later in a different case in California, the Ninth Circuit Court of Appeals did decide to resolve that very same issue.

The official name of that case is *United States vs. Comprehensive Drug Testing* but it has been popularly reported for years as the BALCO case after an alleged steroid dispensary named the Bay Area Laboratory Cooperative. BALCO has been widely alleged to have dispensed anabolic steroids to Barry Bonds and other professional baseball sluggers.

The United States has been vigorously pursuing a law enforcement crusade against anabolic steroids for years. And, after the story broke that the national pastime might have been pharmacologically subverted federal agents joined the witch hunt for steroid using baseball players.

In the course of that witch hunt, the government issued search warrants for the computer records of two independent testing labs, including a firm called Comprehensive Drug Testing. The point of the computer search was to gather evidence against ten big leaguers who were under investigation. But those computer records contained drug tests for ball players and other athletes who were not under investigation. And the records of all those other steroid using athletes were in "plain sight." So the government started investigating all of them.

54

After Alex Rodríguez of the Yankees and David Ortiz of the Red Sox had their names leaked to the press, the Major League Baseball Players Association entered the fight. The player's union objected that the government had conducted an unreasonable search. And on August 31st, the Ninth Circuit agreed with the baseball players.

The Dave Burgess case and the BALCO case could not be less alike except that in both cases the government conducted dragnet searches of computer hard drives in violation of the Fourth Amendment.

The decision in the Comprehensive Drug Testing case has already been widely compared to the *Miranda versus Arizona* decision in 1966. *Miranda* broke ground when it mandated that police must advise suspects of their constitutional rights. In some quarters, Miranda was and still is considered to be a technicality that forces police to coddle criminals. As a matter of fact, *Miranda* ended forced confessions.

Comprehensive Drug Testing, pending Supreme Court review, has just ended dragnet searches of hard drives. The Ninth Circuit has written a set of rules that describe exactly what the police may and may not do when they search your computer or another other device that holds electronically stored information. Today, if you live in any state or territory in the jurisdiction of the Ninth Circuit the following rules apply to computer searches:

1. The Plain View exception no longer applies to computer and other e-forensic searches.
2. Evidence covered in a computer search warrant must be segregated from evidence not specifically described in the warrant. Evidence of new crimes must not be discovered during a computer search. If it is, the e-forensic examiner must keep quiet about it.

3. The method of the government's search protocol must be designed to uncover only the information for which it has probable cause and only that information may be examined by the case agents.

Had Dave Burgess' appeal been heard in San Francisco instead of Denver, he would probably be a free man today.

Arizona Citizen Snaps

It was inevitable. Somebody finally went off on one of Arizona's speeding ticket cameras.

An otherwise law-abiding, good citizen, named Travis Munroe Townsend hit a speeding ticket camera at the corner of 59th Street and the Loop 101 Freeway in suburban Glendale early Thursday morning.

He hit it six times with a pick axe. Arizona State Police caught him in the act. The camera was only slightly damaged and was back in operation by Thursday afternoon.

Townsend, 26, is now incarcerated in the Maricopa County Jail. He is charged with felony criminal damage and interfering with a traffic control device. He faces three years in prison and a $150,000 fine.

Arizona Department of Public Safety (DPS) Director Roger Vanderpool seems intent on making an example out of Townsend. "From criminal damage charges to charges related to interfering with judicial proceedings that can carry lengthy jail terms and hefty fines, the ramifications a person could face for tampering with a photo enforcement site are extremely serious," Vanderpool, or whoever writes his press releases, said. "DPS Officers will continue to be

57

vigilant at all hours of the day and night and stand ready to respond quickly to reports or first hand observances of persons tampering with or vandalizing photo enforcement sites in any manner."

Technically, under Arizona law, a speed limit camera is not a traffic control device. But, Vanderpool apparently interprets Arizona Revised Statute 28-601 to mean that the sign under the camera that reads "Photo Enforced" is a traffic control device. And since the camera is, sort of, attached to the sign by a common pole he construes the camera to be a "traffic control device" as well.

Don't worry. Many people are confused by the subtleties of American law. One of them may even be Roger Vanderpool.

Last month, Vanderpool threatened to use the same charge against the unknown perpetrator or perpetrators who placed yellow sticky notes on the lenses of the automated ticket devices. Those desperados remain unidentified and at large.

The new speeding ticket cameras have been enormously unpopular in Arizona since they were first installed earlier this fall. The machines attempt to capture a photo of the driver and license plate of any car that exceeds the posted speed limit by ten miles an hour or more. The devices have a success rate of about 25 percent.

Still, that was good enough for the DPS to issue 40,401 speeding tickets in the first two months of the "enforcement program." There are about 20 cameras at fixed locations on Phoenix area highways. The DPS plans to install 12 more fixed cameras in Phoenix this month and have 100 cameras in use by the end of January.

Of course, somebody is getting rich off this and it is not the taxpayers. It is the cops and Redflex Traffic

Systems, the company that makes, maintains and actually operates the cameras.

The DPS made $6.6 million off the cameras in two months. Under the normal terms of their contracts, Redflex probably also grossed about $6.6 million off those speeding tickets.

Redflex is an Australian company with U.S. offices in Culver City, California. And, their toll free phone number, by the way, is 866-703-8097 just in case you would like to call them and tell them what you think of the job they are doing.

Usually, Reflex splits the take from the violations it detects with the contracting municipality.

According to a Redflex press release, the company "has contracts with more than 220 U.S. cities, and is the largest provider of digital red light and speed enforcement services in North America. With photo speed programs in 9 states and photo red light programs across 22 states, Redflex has consistently led the market in contract wins, system installation rates and market share."

Karen Finley, CEO of Redflex, brags, "With our US market share rapidly growing, Redflex is unequivocally the most widely trusted name in automated speed enforcement. We are extremely pleased to see the documented benefits to our law enforcement partners who are using Redflex enhanced technologies to significantly decrease the occurrence of speeding, which is one the major causes of crashes, deaths, and injuries on the nation's roadways."

Apparently, CEO is the new spelling for Pirate in Charge.

Numerous Arizona citizens who cannot shake the delusion that America still has something to do with the philosophy of Thomas Jefferson, are outraged by the automated speeding tickets. Some of them have formed a group called Camerafraud which is trying to put an imitative on the Arizona ballot in 2010 to end or soften automated traffic enforcement.

Camerafraud quickly distanced itself from vigilantes like Townsend. In a release, the group said that while attacking the cameras with pickaxes might be emotionally gratifying, it only plays "into the hands of a publicity machine funded by those who profit from photo ticketing."

"It's unfortunate that the person (meaning Townsend) chose not to follow the example of Rosa Parks or Gandhi, both of whom protested against oppressive government by thoughtfully and peacefully breaking the laws they felt to be unjust," the release said.

Great Basin Highway

North Las Vegas is your last chance to buy gas. There is a Shell station on Range Road. If you miss that there is a Mobil on Speedway.

You climb one of the grades that frame the desert cities. Eight percent, maybe ten, for five or six or eight miles. From the summit you can see the Vegas strip poking through the yellow-grey smog. From there it is only another couple of miles to the Route 15, Route 93 split.

Boosters call Route 93 the Great Basin Highway. There is a sign that says that. Old timers call it the Mormon Trail. Whatever you call it, this is where you leave the state of Las Vegas and enter the State of Nevada.

Freighters use this road because it is the fastest route from the Port of Los Angeles up into Idaho – what with the no speed limit and all. Well, technically there is a posted speed limit. It is something like 70 or 75.

But, this is the west bikers know: The used-up west, the poisoned west, the radioactive west, the corrections industry west, the open pit west, the west of bankrupt housing developments. This is the west where the cops leave you alone because when they stop you it is just the two of you. Or, maybe it is the five of you and just the one of him.

Not that any cop is going to sneak up on you. This country is so full of lines and angles and empty spaces the wonder is that the Paiute and the Mojave never invented geometry. There is a fortune in gold lost out there. There has to be. There could be a tribe of Indians hiding out there, a tribe nobody has ever seen. There could be. You could never sneak up on them. They would see you coming.

You can see anything that moves 20 miles away.

I am a good citizen so I start off going 70. Ten minutes later when nothing that I see seems to be getting any closer I look down and discover I am going 80. Then I am clocking 90.

I flash by a car that seems to be crawling. I wait until I see him in my mirrors, signal my lane change, get back over to the right. By then the car is no bigger than my thumbnail and when I look down I am going 105.

The mountains get no closer. I dust off a couple of trucks. I slow down to read a couple of signs.

One sign informs me I am now in Lincoln County. Lincoln County is about twice as big as Connecticut and home to 4,000 souls.

The other sign warns me to watch for low flying aircraft. At first I think the authorities may be drolly warning other motorists about people like me. Then I remember what they call that vast emptiness of Joshua Trees, ocotillo and mesquite over there, over to my left.

People call that Area 51. The aliens have their secret base out there. The government knows all about it but I am not supposed to know. After that, for awhile, I watch the sky but the flying saucers never appear.

Suddenly and unexpectedly the landscape changes. I am in Pahranagat, which is a Paiute word which I am told means shiny lake. I don't speak Paiute so I don't really know. For all I know it means, "The sky aliens left this water for us here."

Pahranagat is a 40 mile long strip of oasis. In 1862, a newspaper reporter named Dan DeQuille wrote a briefly sensational story about the "travelling stones " peculiar to this place.

"Some years ago," DeQuille wrote, "a prospector who had been roaming through the Pahranagat Mountains, the wildest and most sterile portion of southeastern Nevada, brought back with him a great curiosity in the shape of a number of traveling stones. The stones were almost perfectly round, the majority of them as large as a hulled walnut, and very heavy, being of an irony nature. When scattered about on the floor, on a table, or other level surface, within two or three feet of each other, they immediately began traveling toward a common center, and then huddled up in a bunch like a lot of eggs in a nest. A single stone removed to a distance of a yard, upon being released, at once started off with wonderful and somewhat comical celerity to rejoin its fellows; but if taken away four or five feet, it remained motionless."

Eventually, all the lies he had to tell in the course of his chosen profession got to be too much for DeQuille. His problem was he could think them up faster than he could write them down. So he had to hire an assistant. He hired a young man named Samuel Clemens, who began writing under the name Mark Twain. And, eventually Clemens became an even more famous liar than his first editor had been.

Near the end of the Pahranagat you roll into a town called Alamo. The Greater Lincoln County Chamber of Commerce brags that Alamo is a "full service" community. That means it has about three gas stations and a couple of places to eat. About 400 people live there now. Most of them work at the Nevada Test Site.

Unofficially, Alamo is also the iodine isotope 131 capitol of the western world. Alamo was directly downwind from most of the atomic tests in the 1950s and 60s.

In 1956 the New York *Times* cheerfully reported about the tests the previous year: "The heaviest fall-out radiation was 6.93 roentgens recorded in an unpopulated area fifteen miles south of Alamo, Nev. Alamo, on U.S. highway 93, is about sixty miles east of the test area." That might have been the last time Alamo made the New York *Times*.

The year of the real bad tests, a grateful United States of America wrote Alamo a nice letter. "Some of you have been inconvenienced by our test operations," the letter apologized. "At times some of you have been exposed to potential risk from flash, blast, or fall-out. You have accepted the inconvenience or the risk without fuss, without alarm, and without panic."

Alamo, in other words, took one for the country. But, nowhere in the letter does the country ever actually say thank you.

The government eventually paid off each of the people who got cancer and who were not yet dead from it with a one time only, lump sum payment of $50,000.

I get off the bike and gas up in town and have a pleasant conversation with a real nice, tough looking guy who is riding a Big Dog.

"That sure is a pretty bike."

"Thanks."

"Isn't it hard to ride that thing?"

"Not really. Not when I'm going straight. It's only tough to turn. Do you know how far it is to Tonapah?" He has pretty big ears and a shaved head. At one time, I believe he had plugs in his ears but he must have lost them somewhere because now there are just the holes.

"I know it's a ways."

"I came up from Vegas. I want to ride over to Tonapah then head down through Beatty and get home that way."

I lend him my maps. I always have maps. We calculate it is about 155 or 165 miles between gas stations the way he wants to go.

He has no saddlebags or any of the crap I carry in mine —maps, water, chewing gum, rain suit, sweat shirt, candy, GPS, tool kit, tire repair kit and a snake bite kit. I started carrying the snake bite kit after a close call with a rattlesnake.

My new friend carries none of this. Carrying the crap I carry would mar the exquisite lines of his beautiful bike.

The two of us ride out of town sort of together and sort of alone at the same time. After a dozen miles he turns left onto Route 375, the "extraterrestrial highway." He waves. I wave. We both have understated, masculine waves.

He told me back in town that his bike would only go about 140 miles on a tank. And, I thought we had agreed that he couldn't make it all the way to Tonopah before he ran dry. But he just still has to try it anyway. I like his attitude.

There he goes.

Maybe he got back to Vegas that night. Maybe he got adopted by an Indian tribe nobody has ever seen. Maybe, a hundred years from now he will return from a voyage to the stars and he will not have aged a day. Anything can happen out here.

The Pahranagat yields to a network of sandstone canyons and after only another 55 or 60 miles I roll into the old railhead at Caliente. The railroad came through in 1905 and by 1910 Caliente was already the biggest town in Lincoln County. It had a population of 1,755. Now it is down to only about two-thirds of that but it is still the biggest place I have seen since I got on the 93.

There is water in Caliente. Water is the future of Caliente. Water is what is going to bring people back. The water in Caliente is a dream of a golf course and a resort and a brand new housing development. Of course, La Vegas wants Caliente's water, too. Las Vegas has its own dreams.

Twenty-five or thirty miles north of Caliente is Pioche. It is named for Francois Pioche who owned the town after the Civil War. In the 1870s it was the toughest town in the west. Deadwood was Disneyland. Pioche was Khe Sanh.

Pioche was a silver mining town. The old tram for the ore buckets still stretches over the highway. And in the boom days there was no law. So, there was no way to hold a silver claim except to be quick with a gun or hire somebody who was. The hired guns streamed in from all over the west. Seventy-five men died in showdowns before anybody in Pioche died a natural death.

The silver played out in 1876 but Pioche bided its time. Sure enough, in the 1940s Pioche rose again to become America's second largest producer of lead and zinc. Then the Second World War ended and America found itself some other place to get its lead and zinc.

Pioche still has, to the best of my knowledge, one gas pump, two restaurants and three saloons. The saloon I enter has a cherry wood bar that came around South America on a sailing ship. I can imagine how it got to San Francisco but I cannot imagine how this bar got from San Francisco to here. None of my mid-afternoon drinking companions knows either. Actually, none of them gives a damn.

All I know is that in the best of times in Pioche nobody thought this town needed a sheriff. But everybody agreed that Pioche needed a real nice bar.

For 110 miles north of Pioche the long straight road cuts mostly through a savanna thick with sage. Here and there on the high spots are the pinon and juniper scrub that you see all over the west. Mostly there is ancient sage thick as hedge.

This is what geographers call the Great Basin Desert. There are three deserts in the west: The Mojave which sometimes features Joshua Trees; the Colorado which has Saguaros; and this place which is dominated by sage. People call this a desert but by now the temperature has already dropped down into the 80s and as I ride along I amuse myself by thinking about whether this is really a desert or not.

Eventually I conclude that this place has way to many bugs to be a desert. Every mile four or five of them commit suicide on my face. Although, I have to admit some of them may not be bugs at all. Some of them may be very small birds.

I am worried enough about running out of gas that I am only going about 85. Most places, 85 is enough to make me the fastest thing on the road anyway. But this afternoon as I glance in my mirrors I am surprised to discover that I am about to be passed. Someone in a little, red, boxy, piece of crap runs past me going about a hundred.

I pass the time watching him disappear. I am bored. I wonder how far I have to go but I won't look at my odometer. I know I will get there faster if I do not count the miles.

I watch the speeding, red, piece of crap grow smaller instead. When I cannot see him anymore, I promise myself, I will look down to see how far I have come. And, when I finally look down I am about 50 miles north of Pioche.

Steady does it, I coach myself.

Although, I don't get passed on this kind of road very often. So, I have to ruminate on that for a few miles. Am I slowing down? Am I no longer the motorcyclist I once was?

Well, shit. Of course I am not. Shit.

Then up ahead, by the side of the road, I see the little red box. I brake and downshift.

I am a good Samaritan is what the hell I am. As God is my witness. Most of the time if you are broken down I can't do a damn thing for you. But, I will at least stop and talk and try to cheer you up. I will do my best to give you false hope. I will do that much.

Two young men who are both about the same age I was the first time I had to kill somebody, the first time I knew I was going to die, are pulling their luggage out of their trunk. It has not yet occurred to either of them that they are ever going to die.

"Are you guys, alright?"

"No," the one without a beard says. "It stop! Poof!" He looks like a character in a Judd Apatow film. There is no beautiful starlet though, only the other young man. This ain't the movies. They are German I think.

"Do you have gas?"

"Poof," he says again.

"You have phone," the other one asks me. He looks stupid and mean. He might be dangerous if he put on another 50 pounds.

"No partner. Cell phones don't work out here."

"Poof," the beardless idiot laughs.

"You have phone?" The idiot with the beard pantomimes using a phone for me.

"Listen pal. Pioche is about 55 miles back there." I jerk my thumb. "Ely is about 55 miles up ahead." I stab my finger. "This is a bad place to break down." I smirk. "Did you run out of gas." I raise my eyebrows as inquisitively as possible.

But, my sign language is no good. "Poof! Ha, ha, ha!"

"There has to be a truck back behind me, somewhere." I know they do not understand a word I say but I talk anyway. "When you see him you flag him down. He'll have a radio."

"Poof!"

"And stay out of that sage. Jesus. Snakes in that sage."

"You have phone?"

I twist the throttle and take off. I leave them there. I speak only slightly more German than I speak Paiute so I cannot even cheer them up.

I don't want to cheer them up, anyway. I want to tell them this is not Vegas. This is not the country with cell phones. This is the American west. I want to tell them this but I know they would not understand.

Deadly And Delicious

The deer call these late fall days "motorcycle hunting season."

The end of October and beginning of November is mating season in the deer world. Whether you can see them or not, if you are riding a country road they see you. They are standing just inside the tree line, getting drunk on fermented berries. And, by the time they see you they are either giddy from their latest sexual conquest or despondent over the fact that, once again, it is closing time they are leaving that fermented berry patch all alone.

Maybe the giddy ones feel invincible. Maybe the despondent ones are committing suicide. Some people even claim that deer are just stupid on the subject of highways.

For whatever reason, if you are one of those people who insist on reasons, about ten motorcycle-deer collisions made the news in the last week which means that there were probably 20 more that did not make the news.

About a third of the collisions were fatal and there is nothing funny about them. Every single motorcycle fatality is tragic to someone.

On the other hand, some of the non-fatal collisions are sort of droll.

For example, last Tuesday night Michael Reed, 57, of Canandaigua, NY was riding west on the New York Thruway between Exits 42 and 43 when a deer ran out in front him, stopped, froze and glared with that arrogant glare that drunk, horny deer have. Reed braked but he could not stop in time and wound up hitting the deer.

The deer died. Reed lived.

Reed suffered what were described as "facial and leg injuries" and a riding companion called 911. The ambulance arrived, picked up Reed and headed for the nearest hospital, Clifton Springs.

A doctor at that hospital, however, cautioned the paramedics that Reed might have a head injury. So, in mid-course the ambulance diverted to a bigger hospital in Rochester.

Which was about the time the ambulance hit another drunken, horny deer. The ambulance sustained a crumpled hood and a broken grill and headlight and was determined to be undrivable.

So a second ambulance was called. And, that emergency vehicle managed to get Reed to a hospital without colliding with yet another deer. But, it does say something telling about the mood the deer are in these days that it took two tries.

Reed was listed as being in satisfactory condition the next day, by the way. If you live in Rochester send him a card. And, whatever you do, watch out for them deer.

According to the State Farm Insurance Company "deer-related vehicle collisions have risen almost 6% from the last deer season." State Farm policy holders have run into 192,877 deer in the last year.

Ten states: Pennsylvania, Michigan, Illinois, Ohio, Georgia, Virginia, Minnesota, Texas, Indiana and South Carolina account for slightly more than half of all the accidents reported to State Farm. And, the time when these accidents are most likely to occur is at dusk and at night.

One of the problems motorcyclists have with deer is that experienced bikers instinctively do the wrong thing. Somewhere along the line, everybody learns the maxim that "to avoid an obstacle you should swerve by executing a sharp counter steer." Yeah, right.

Motorcycle "safety courses" always teach this. When you see the pile of bricks fall off the truck in front of you just push one of your grips hard. It does not matter which way you go. Just push as hard as you can and trust the bike to veer you around the obstacle.

But, when you see a deer the last thing you want to do is counter steer because when you move the deer moves. And riding across the road increases your chances of hitting a tree, a ditch or a fence even if you miss the deer. So whatever you do, don't counter steer. Try to brake to a stop, but if you have to hit the deer hit the deer as squarely as possible.

Two more bits of advice. Deer whistles do not work. And if you kill the deer you get to eat it. Whether you have a hunting license or not, in most states the meat still belongs to you. The meat, the antlers and the skin, the whole damn thing, is all yours.

So be careful and enjoy your barbeque.

Bikers Still Menace

The police still fear us. They still really, really fear us.

Let's face it, okay? The reason why some of you ride a large, loud, patriotic motorcycle; have multiple tattoos; wear work clothes and black leather to the mall; carry a knife and maybe a gun; glare at strangers; and wear your wallet on a chain is because you know it makes all those guys who think they are better than you wet their pants.

For the rest of us the intimidation factor is probably at least a fringe benefit. Yet, an argument still rages over the true nature of the biker soul.

On one side, Harley-Davidson and its dealers and the big event promoters and many snide, GenX journalists all argue that most bikers are really just wealthy dentists unwinding from a hard week at the drill. Look, it's only Harleyween; the AARP on motorcycles; RUBs; Rolex Riders; poseurs; bank presidents, CEOs and lawyers! There is nothing to fear from them except maybe a lawsuit! Raise the prices on everything!

And then the responsible opposing view, that smart bikers are psychopaths and stupid bikers are animals, can be heard at any Myrtle Beach City Council meeting or read in any of the multiplying tales about the heroic deeds of heroic Jay Dobyns. Biker America! With special guest stars, the Pagans Motorcycle Club on a Saturday night! The sub-culture that is so violent that even the motorcycle missionaries will cap your ass, cut you up with a Bowie knife and bury the pieces in the desert!

Harmless biker or dangerous biker? What do the police think? In a couple of recent instances in California real, live bikers have given local police a bad case of the shakes.

March 8, the Vagos Motorcycle Club held a fundraiser to help pay the bills of a member who has cancer. The Vagos charged admission, provided food and sold tee-shirts. All the women kept their tops on. If you are reading this now the chances are pretty good that you have been to at least a couple dozen similar runs.

Vagos, friends of the Vagos, independent bikers, Harley Owner's Group members, Rich Urban Bikers and others rode into a politely remote Veterans of Foreign Wars Post, VFW Post 6110 on the Sierra Highway in a southern California town called Canyon Country. Police estimated the crowd at "more than" 300.

"This was a family event. Riders came with their wives and children," VFW Commander John Olish said. But the police felt forced to push their weight around anyway.

Various special police units including the Los Angeles County Sheriff's COBRA Team (COBRA stands for Career Offenders Burglary Robbery Apprehension), the Community Interaction Team, the Community Oriented Policing Services Unit and another dozen patrol and traffic officers, all under the most excellent command of a Sheriff's Captain named Anthony La Berge "broke up" what news accounts described as an "outlaw biker gang event."

74

A road block was established to trap any bikers who might try to escape and about thirty, or one in ten of the participants, were hit with some charge. Charges included failure to carry proof of insurance, illegally high handlebars, failure to stop, disturbing the peace and failure to obey a police officer. Some Vagos prospects, who halted traffic to allow bikes to safely enter or exit the event were cited for impeding traffic.

A Sheriff's spokesman named Sergeant Darren Harris, explained that "Although the gathering itself is not unlawful, some of the actions of these individuals and the motorcycles they are riding are illegal. Not to mention the fact that they can be disruptive to the peace and serenity of the community. Our primary goal is to ensure public safety and peace in response to community complaints and concerns about these bikers. We will do whatever it takes to accomplish just that." In other words, bikers are scary.

Then about a week ago, the police in a crappy little town east of Fresno, named Sanger, decided to make an example out of five members of the Vietnam Vets Motorcycle Club and the Legacy Vets MC. Two of the riders that day, Glen Webster and George Swigart are disabled veterans with the proper paperwork to park in a handicapped space. Webster got blown up by a hand grenade while serving with the First Air Cav in 1968. Swigart is a Vietnam era Navy veteran. One of the Legacy Vets just returned from Iraq.

All five of them parked their motorcycles in one disabled parking space. Their reasoning was that two of them earned the right to park there. And, the polite thing to do was to only use one space to park all of the bikes.

The five were almost immediately surrounded by seven cops including a gang officer and a member of the local SWAT Team. All five were issued $900 tickets for illegal parking and urged to move on.

Webster, who has a young wife and two children, told the Fresno *Bee* that he cannot afford to pay the fine. "They're gonna have to throw me in jail," he told the *Bee*. "I'm not gonna pay $900 out of my family's budget. If I'm in jail, I still get my veteran's administration benefits."

Webster and Swigart are both in their sixties. And, if there is bright side to this it is that they are still frightening small town cops.

Sioux Falls Defense Rests

The defense rested Monday in the Sioux Falls, South Dakota trial of two Hells Angels accused of shooting five people in a motel parking lot in Custer State Park about 70 miles south of Sturgis during the Black Hills Rally in 2006.

The defense took less than two days to complete and called just four witnesses. The prosecution called 43 witnesses in seven and a half days.

The defendants are Chad Wilson, 33, a patched member of the San Diego Chapter of the Hells Angels Motorcycle Club and Haney , British Columbia HA prospect John Midmore, 35. Wilson admits shooting Thomas Hass, Al Mathews, Danny Neace, Claudia Wables and Susan Evans-Martin. The three men are members of the American Outlaw Association (AOA), which is commonly called the Outlaws Motorcycle Club.

The Angels and the Outlaws began a blood feud in April, 1974 when members of the AOA allegedly killed three Hells Angels in Florida. In the last 34 years the feud has never been completely resolved. Outlaws, for example, still sometimes wear a club-only patch that reads ADIOS, an acronym for Angels Die In Outlaw States.

Wilson and Midmore's defense was, in essence, that they were innocent victims of Outlaws intent on perpetuating this vendetta. The prosecution's case stands on the assertion that the Outlaws and their two female companions were innocent tourists victimized by an unprovoked Hells Angels drive-by shooting. Both sides concede that everybody was carrying big bore automatic handguns.

Integral to the defense, was police intelligence that indicated that members of the Outlaws intended to attack members of the Hells Angels during the Black Hills Rally at Sturgis that year. The defense asked the jury to believe that the two defendants were aware of this police intelligence and so they had a reasonable fear of members of the AOA.

The last prosecution witness was Danny Neace, a member of the AOA from Michigan who is under indictment for attacking a member of the Hells Angels. And, in its opening statement the defense harped on Neace's refusal to answer questions about this alleged attack. Defense attorney David Kenner told the jury that, "That hostile mind-set that you heard from Mr. Neace and others permeated this group of Outlaws...this high-ranking group of Outlaws."

The defense then called its first witness, a "professor of animation" named James Tavernetti, who showed the jury a cartoon. Over the repeated objections of Prosecutor Michael Moore, Judge Gene Kean allowed the presentation.

So the jury saw a cartoon Chad Wilson, prevented by traffic and cartoon Outlaws in front of and behind his cartoon truck, where the two cartoon Hells Angels were "sitting ducks," getting out and firing a cartoon gun in defense of his life.

The prosecutor then futilely cross-examined the animation professor, but since the professor was not actually at the scene of the shooting he had little to add to the prosecution's case except to agree that in the cartoon, it sure looked like the Hells Angels had room to escape.

The defense then called psychologist Thomas Streed who testified that any competent psychologist could see that obviously the defendant's action were spontaneous and not premeditated. The psychologist observed that the shooting took place in a crowded parking lot with police near by, that the defendants had apparently given no thought to escape and that they were eating ice cream at the time.

Streed told the jury that the prosecution's theory of the crime was fatuous. "I see spontaneity and absolutely no evidence of planning," Streed testified. "Why would you bring ice cream to a gunfight?"

This expert witness also made the prosecution look slightly less than highly qualified during cross-examination. Moore dared the psychologist to explain the discrepancy between statements made by witnesses and the defendants. So Streed did. He implied that the witnesses were intimidated by the Outlaws. "Witness statements are always problematic in biker cases," he testified.

The defense then called Michael Baden, a forensic pathologist who has appeared on a show called *Autopsy* on *HBO*. And, he testified that the victims injuries were consistent with Wilson's statements.

Finally Chad Wilson took the stand in his own defense.

He told the jury that he and his co-defendant Midmore were driving to a strip club when they stopped near the shooting scene to smoke a joint. Wilson went into a store to buy snacks and water and discovered that he had stumbled into a nest of Outlaws. He hurried back out to the truck to escape but it was too late. His Hells Angels tattoos had given him away.

According to Wilson, the two men tried to drive away but were prevented by traffic, and possibly the effects of the dope, from getting out of the lot and onto the road. When Outlaws surrounded them Wilson got out. One outlaw who was not injured, named Nathan Frazier pulled a gun and dropped it. Another Outlaw named Lon Baillargeon pulled a gun and fired at Wilson. "I was terrified," Wilson told the jury. "There's nine of them, two of us."

Wilson said he then pulled an automatic pistol out of his belt, crouched and shot back as Frazier bent over to pick up his gun. "One thing led to another and it didn't stop. If I didn't shoot back, they were going to keep shooting at me until I was dead."

Neither Frasier and Baillargeon were hit by the admittedly stoned Wilson's fire.

After about four seconds, Wilson testified, he got back in the truck and escaped.

During cross-examination, the prosecutor argued that Wilson's shooting of five other people who the defendant admitted were not actually shooting at him while missing the two men he claimed were actually shooting at him was proof of premeditation rather than intoxication.

After Wilson and Midmore's escape, they discarded the gun Wilson had used in the shooting along the road. After deciding that no one was following them, the two threw away two other guns on a logging trail and then abandoned their truck. Eventually, they were arrested by a Custer State Park ranger named James Laverick.

In his closing remarks, the prosecutor emphasized that Wilson shot five people so obviously he was shooting. But nobody had shot him or his truck so it would be reasonable to conclude that nobody was shooting at him. And, the prosecutor told the jury that numerous eye-witnesses supported his logic. The witnesses all "agree that the Outlaws were not the aggressors," he said.

The case is now in the hands of the jury and a verdict may be reached as early as Wednesday.

HA Trademark Suit

Someday, maybe a whole week will go by without the Hells Angels Motorcycle Club making headlines. Maybe next week. This one is just too good.

The Hells Angels Motorcycle Corporation, a California corporation, is suing a Visalia, California woman named Fawn Myers; a man named Terry Myers; the Arizona based web host GoDaddy.com.; and ten John Does for cyberpiracy; trademark infringement; false description of origin; dilution; and unfair competition. The Angels are also demanding a jury trial.

The lawsuit was initiated on February 10, filed in the Federal Eastern District of California Court in Fresno on the 11 and became public yesterday after John Ellis of the Fresno *Bee* broke the story.

The Hells Angels Motorcycle Corporation (HAMC) is described in the suit as, "a non-profit mutual benefit corporation organized and existing under the laws of the State of California." "Authorized charters of the Hells Angels Motorcycle Club" are described as "licensees" of the corporation.

The Angels, as everyone but our Martian friends know, have long been associated with both the initials HA and the number 81. The HAMC maintains that both have been trademarks of the corporation for "over twenty years." For any Martians that make it onto the jury, the suit also explains that, "Plaintiff's '81' mark is a numeric metonym for the initials 'H' and 'A' which are the 8th and 1st letters of the English alphabet, thereby signifying Hells Angels."

Ms. Myers, the defendant, is described as "engaged in (the) business of buying and selling collectible items and domain name registrations, primarily through the internet auction site eBay.com…."

And, Myers is now being sued because on February 7 she offered 20 domain names for sale. The domains had all been registered with GoDaddy.com and all the domains incorporated either "HA" or "81."

The full list of domains Myers registered with GoDaddy includes: HAMC.COM; HA-MC.INFO; ALL81.COM; USA81.COM; 81USA.COM; 81-MC.COM; 81USA.INFO; 81-MC.INFO; 81MC.INFO; 81AZ.COM; 81CA.COM; 81CT.COM; 81EU.COM; 81FL.COM; 81HI.COM; 81NJ.COM; 81NV.COM; 81NY.COM; 81OC.COM; 81TX.COM; 81UT.COM; and 81WA.COM.

On eBay, Myers explained that she hadn't made the association between the abbreviation HA and the metonym 81 when she registered the domains, only shortly before she decided to sell them. "I was contacted by a person outside the United States interested in purchasing 81EU.com for a European web site," Myers told potential buyers. She explained, "A brandable four or five letter dot com domain name now days (sic) goes for $3800 all the way to $1,000,000 +."

And, in her eBay pitch, Myers also reveals that she understands that HA is a "brand," by which she seems to mean a trademark, of the Hells Angels. "First off, I would like to say I have no HA affiliation," she says right at the beginning, using the disputed mark "HA" to mean Hells Angels.

The corporate Hells Angels told eBay to stop the auction on February 8. The online auction site complied. Myers then offered the domain names for sale by auction on GoDaddy. And, that is what prompted the Angels' suit.

The suit asks that Myers, GoDaddy and any as yet unnamed business partners be enjoined from selling the domains: that the defendants should forfeit any profits Myers has already made; and that Myers, who probably does not have any money and GoDaddy which certainly does, should be liable for $2 million actual damages and triple that amount in punitive damages.

Really, Myers doesn't stand a chance. Right off the bat, she is blatantly in violation of a Federal statute that outlaws bad faith attempts to profit from domain names that would most logically be associated with someone else.

Even if it were available, for example, it would be illegal to register something like HarleyDavidson.com with the intent of eventually selling that domain back to the motorcycle manufacturer. It is called "cyber squatting" and it as illegal as identity theft.

Terry Myers, told the *Bee* that he and Fawn Myers are the real victims. He protested that the domain HAMC.ORG is registered to the Hebrew Academy of Morris County, New Jersey and the name HAMC.COM is owned by the Heart of America Medical Center in Rugby, North Dakota. He implies that if the Hells Angels are allowed to win this suit they will probably be going after Hebrew schools and Medical centers next.

Which raises another obvious question. What do you think the odds are that this guy graduated from Harvard Law? Or do you think he learned most of what he knows about the lawsuits from TV?

Myers also told the *Bee* that he has already tried to give the domain names to the Hells Angels as a gift if they will just agree to withdraw their suit. But so far nobody has called him back.

Hi Yo Silver

This is why people hate yuppies.

Six weeks ago, the RPA advertising agency of Santa Monica, on behalf of the Honda Motor Company of Japan, thought it would be "groovy" if they could throw videos up on the web of a real, actual stretch of road playing a song when a Honda Civic drove over it.

Isn't that the most fabulous idea, uh...Topher? Jago? Julian? Allegra? Apparently Topher, Jago, Julian and Allegra all agreed. "Hey, we know! Let's call it "experiential marketing!"

Subsequently, RPA and Honda, had a set of grooves of different heights cut in Avenue K in the high desert town of Lancaster in far northern Los Angeles County. The ad campaign was called, "Honda Civic: A 'Groovy' Kind of Car."

How does that sound?

Long ago, the post-modern icon John Barth wrote that "there are things worth doing and things worth remarking." And the groovy road, unless you are the kind of yuppie dog who works for an ad agency, self-evidently qualifies as one of those "creative" things that it is perfectly fine to "brainstorm" about as long as you don't actually go out into some desert town and do it.

The web site Autopia called it the "Most Annoying Promotion Ever." Honda, of course, or one of their barking yuppie dogs, renamed the quarter mile stretch of black top "Civic Musical Road" because when you drove or rode over it it played the best known bars of The William Tell Overture by Gioachino Rossini. You know that song. It is the theme from the 1950s television series *The Lone Ranger*.

One little barking dog yapped that the song sounded best when the road was run over by a "brand new" Honda Civic going "exactly" 55-miles-an-hour. Next thing you know, one of these insufferably precious little parasites is going to proclaim that this is why all those guys died in Vietnam.

And, for the record, it does make a sound when you ride over it on a motorcycle. Doesn't sound like Rossini though. On a motorcycle it sounds more like a banshee.

After 18 days of this, local residents were finally able to convince their local government to please, for God's sake, make this terrible noise stop! "When you hear it late at night, it will wake you up from a sound sleep. It's awakened my wife three or four times a night," Lancaster resident Brian Robin said.

"We thought it was far enough away," Antelope Valley Film Office liaison Pauline East added.

After all, the road is in a remote area. And who in their right mind would move to a remote area for the quiet?

The grooves were paved over on September 24th.

And predictably, the respite was brief. Guess what happened next. The grooves won. Money won.

Lancaster City Hall was "flooded" with hundreds of "requests" to bring back the "musical road." Some calls came from "Canada." Just think about that for a minute. Canada. And, now you can go ahead and make up your own punch line.

"There's been an overwhelming positive response from both citizens and the nation at large. It's captured people's imaginations," Lancaster Mayor R. Rex Parris told *The Associated Press*, before adding the same pathetic excuse every town in the world makes just before it soils itself. "It will be a tourist attraction. It will pull people off the freeway."

Last week the Lancaster City Council actually appropriated $35,000 to cut new grooves into a new street. The new grooves will still play the same old song when people drive over them. The city hired the same company that cut the original grooves. So they get to do the same job twice.

There has been, as yet, no report of what the members of the Lancaster City Council got from Honda or the ad agency or the groove cutting company except for the satisfaction that always comes from a job well done.

The new musical road will be a stretch of Avenue G in Lancaster, between 30th and 40th Streets West.

Shush. Hear that? Know what that sound is? That's right. That's the sound of all those Canadians with all their Canadian dollars pouring into Lancaster.

Lancaster Boots Mongols

In such movie classics as *Son of Frankenstein*, *Ghost of Frankenstein* and *Frankenstein Meets the Wolf Man* all that is good, pure and true in life is saved from despoliation at the hands of a semi-human monster by an angry lynch mob. Well the newest version is called *Frankenstein's Motorcycle Club* and the role of the monster is now being played by the Mongols Motorcycle Club.

The Mongols had planned their national run for this weekend in the Los Angeles adjacent, high desert community of Lancaster. Lancaster is famous for wind, scorpions and the world famous Lancaster Musical Road. The musical road is left over from a Honda commercial. Or rather, it is an amazing reconstruction of something left over from a Honda commercial. When you ride over them a series of grooves cut in the road make a terrible noise that is supposed to resemble the William Tell Overture.

In years past the Mongols have retired to places like Palm Springs for their national run but the club is a little down on its luck this year so they rented out all 144 rooms of a fifth rate motel called the Desert Inn in Lancaster. Reviews of the Desert inn are generally very, very bad.

"I have stayed in some bad motels over the years but I have to say this one is at the top of the list. Of course I stayed at the Desert Inn to try to save some money but honestly I was better of sleeping in my car," one reviewer begins on TripAdvisor.com. Others call the motel "The Desert Dump."

Then Lancaster's flamboyant mayor, R. Rex Parris – he who dreamed the magnificent dream of the musical road – found out the Mongols were coming. Parris convened a secret meeting with the Lancaster City Council Tuesday night. When he came out he warned the waiting reporters, who had been excluded from the "public meeting," that the Mongols were coming and explained who the Mongols are.

"The Mongols are the ones that had the gang fight with the Hells Angels in Laughlin, and there were murders there," he explained to a reporter for the Lancaster *Valley Press*. "They are a bad gang, and we are not going to become a recreational area for outlaw motorcycle gangs ever."

Yesterday Parris made good on his threat. Los Angeles County Sheriff's Deputies, playing the role of the lynch mob, officially closed the Desert Inn and erected a chain link fence around the place.

"We received word that the Mongols outlaw motorcycle club was going to have a convention here at the Desert Inn," a Sheriff named Axel Anderson explained. "They probably, right now, are the most powerful outlaw motorcycle group in Southern California."

City Manager Mark Bozigian explained that the motel was past due on hotel bed tax payments. Then he said that "the prospect of the Mongols motorcycle gang coming up here and renting the whole hotel…hastened the prosecution of this case."

Mayor Parris explained that Lancaster had been trying to help the financially troubled motel stay in business for several months. When the Desert Inn refused to cancel the Mongols reservations, the city decided to shut the place down. The Mongols, "are engaged in domestic terrorism," Parris explained, "and they kill our children."

Albert Perez, Jr., an attorney who was authorized to speak on behalf of the Mongols, said the club would sue if the Desert Inn reopened next week.

Lars Wilson Flipped

On October 14, 2007, in a recorded conversation on a cell phone the ATF called "Target telephone 3," former Mongols Motorcycle Club President Ruben "Doc" Cavazos told his former "right hand man," Robert Lawrence "Lars" Wilson III to "man up" and "be a leader."

The two are still partners in the same dance. Cavazos is still leading. Wilson still following. Cavazos entered into a plea and sentencing agreement with the Department of Justice on January 23rd. Wilson pled guilty to running a racket on March 27th. He pled guilty to something else on June 9th.

This week Wilson is scheduled to be transported by United States Marshalls from a currently undisclosed location to the Federal Correctional Institution (FCI) in Elkton, Ohio "to wait until his sentence or" until he is "called to testify against other defendants in the case. In addition, Mr. Wilson has information which may be useful to local law enforcement in Indiana, who will be better able to meet with him and the case agent if he is held in Ohio."

FCI Elkton is a "low security facility housing male offenders" near Lisbon, Ohio. The prison is about 30 miles south of Youngstown, and 45 miles northwest of Pittsburgh, Pennsylvania.

The fact that Wilson pled to an additional charge last month and that he is still remembering things Federal agents find interesting proves the ongoing nature of this case. An indication of the size, scope and momentum of this investigation is that it has gotten too big to hide it all. Information has begun to appear in plain sight like rocks falling out of a glacier.

Lars Wilson and Doc Cavazos spent endless hours chatting on the phone like school girls. And, their numerous conversations have the surreal quality of a Steely Dan song. Something like "Pretzel Logic."

As Wilson was about to fly to Philly to "promote the club" Cavazos complained that everyone was trying to "whack" him and that the club was full of "traitors." Wilson sympathized. Then a few months later on February 8, 2008, Wilson and Shawn Buss discussed their plans to seize control of the club from Doc.

Doc "participates" in the writing of his memoir. Doc talks to the History Channel's *Gangland* "reality show," chats about murders with a reporter and negotiates with *HBO* to produce a documentary about him and his club. Meanwhile, a pole camera watches as Cavazos parades back and forth in front of his house carrying a rifle - waiting for his very many enemies, ready to go mano a mano with the dreaded Gage Maravilla or the Avenues or the Eme or the HA.

After September 7, 2007 video cameras and microphones installed in his home recorded every belch. Every word on his cell phone and land line were recorded. His son's cell phone recorded every word he said. And, as Wilson was bragging that he planned to patch in 1,000 new Mongols at Daytona and take Florida away from the Warlocks and the Outlaws. Lil' Rubes girlfriend was having coffee with ATF Special Agent John Ciccone.

The Feds knew when Wilson travelled to Daytona on October 20, 2007 to buy guns from the Outlaws. The Feds were listening when Cavazos and Wilson discussed using those guns to "take out" the Outlaws.

The Feds were listening on August 1st and September 13th, 2007 as the Mongols plotted and partied and bragged with the Pagans Motorcycle Club. The Feds were listening on January 10th, 2008 as Wilson ordered Mongols to drive the Pagans out of Baltimore.

Ciccone was listening as Wilson warned Doc about the formation of a "brotherhood" between the Bandidos and the Sons of Silence. They listened as he counted 20 members of the Henchmen Motorcycle Club in Gary, Indiana. And they were listening as Doc bragged back that everyone in California had to "recognize" him because "the state belongs to the Mongols."

The Feds are still listening to both of them because they are both still talking. No wonder *HBO* was willing to pay for a piece of this.

East LA Saturday Night

Now morons are lighting up family clubs.

Three people were killed and seven more were wounded when an unknown gunman opened fire on a "family and friends event" called "Old School Bike Night" being held at Falcone's Pizza on Slauson Avenue in Pico Rivera. The flyer for the event promised "Good Food. Good Music. Lots of Fun. Security will be provided for bikes and cars." Pico Rivera is east of downtown Los Angeles.

It could have been worse. At least twelve children were present at the event. The Old School Riders describe themselves as, "just ordinary people who enjoy the freedom of riding. No one represents any club. We are just friends and family who gather together and ride. Safety is our main concern for everyone who rides with us."

Three men were killed and seven people were wounded. Three of the wounded were women.

Police refused to say how many gunmen were involved. Eyewitnesses say they saw two gunmen, two drivers and two cars. Published reports identify two of the dead men as Gerret Dandini and his cousin, Tony Dandini.

Detective Joe Sheehy of the Los Angeles County Sheriff's Homicide Bureau has been quoted by several news sources as suggesting that the attack was actually aimed at the Mongols Motorcycle Club but somebody shot up the wrong event. "If this was (an attack) against Mongols, it was definitely a case of mistaken identity," Sheehy told Brian Day of the San Gabriel Valley *News*.

At the time of the shootings in Pico Rivera, the Mongols were actually being closely watched by officers from five police departments and agents from the Bureau of Alcohol, Tobacco, Firearms and Explosives (ATF).

Last week the Azusa, California Police Department issued a "tactical alert" that the Mongols were planning a party at a restaurant on Foothill Boulevard, old Route 66, in Azusa. When the partiers arrived they were greeted by a command center and officers from the Montebello, Azusa, Glendora, Arcadia and Monrovia Police departments. The Mongols and friends were also surveilled by a Los Angeles County Sherriff's Department helicopter.

A source has alleged that ATF Case Agent John Ciccone and another well known "outlaw motorcycle gang investigator" named Chris Cervantes both attended the event with their special spy cameras. Cervantes works for the Montebello police and his hobbies include the Mongols.

Meanwhile, a couple of miles away, innocent families were being gunned down.

Special Memory Knife Fight

A knife fight broke out at the "A Special Memory Wedding Chapel" in downtown Las Vegas late Saturday after the chapel manager inadvertently scheduled a Mongols Motorcycle Club wedding ceremony right after a Hells Angels Motorcycle Club wedding ceremony.

The wedding chapel's owner, Joshua Gust, told Las Vegas television station *KTNV* that the knife fight was just bad luck. "There's 100,000 weddings a year in Las Vegas and how many across the world. To have two groups that close together, I think that is very odd," Gust said.

The Hells Angels, Mongols and the Bandidos Motorcycle Club all have club houses in Las Vegas. Most people understand that the three clubs do not attend each other's weddings.

"We were friggin' attacked," the groom, an unidentified Mongol told the Vegas television station. "We defended ourselves the best we could. It's real hard to do when you are outnumbered that bad. But that is alright." The groom was stabbed three times in the stomach. The best man was also stabbed. The bride was not harmed.

"I would like to say, the police and certain people are putting it out there that we did something wrong," the groom added. "That's not what it is. I came here to get married. I didn't even know that other people were here."

Las Vegas Metro Police have confirmed that the fight occurred but, as is the custom with police, refuse to release even the most basic details of the brawl including the two clubs involved, the names of the combatants or the extent of their injuries.

"We have some video that we are reviewing," Metro Police Lieutenant Richard Fletcher admitted reluctantly. "It won't be released at this time. It has been turned over to detectives."

It was the Mongols and the Angels, sir. Okay? Everybody already knows. Two Mongols were stabbed.

A Special Memory Wedding Chapel, at 800 South Fourth Street, is one of the classier chapels in Vegas. It is in a building that looks like an old New England church. It seats about 90 people, in case you want to bring your whole club, and as is usual in Vegas, you can buy a bridal veil, flowers, photos, a cake and champagne on site.

A Special Memory also features a drive-up window if you are in a hurry and want to get the ceremony over with before one of you sobers up. The chapel does three hundred drive-up weddings a month. The drive up weddings only cost $25 but the souvenir tee-shirt costs extra.

Whores Will Save Vegas

Bad girls. We talking about bad girls. Bad girls are going to save Las Vegas.

Perhaps you had not realized that Las Vegas needs to be saved. But, oh yes. Vegas changed man. And, then it all went bad. Real bad.

In the good old days, Las Vegas was always showy and glitzy and intentionally cheap. Snobs called it tacky. Common men called it classy.

Benny Binion opened the Horseshoe in 1951, invented the World Series of Poker and made a few dollars in Vegas. And, Benny once said that the secret to his success was that he made "little people feel like big people."

Jay Samo, who built Ceasars Palace with $10 million he happened to find just sitting there, in the Teamsters Central States Pension Fund, called his joint Caesars because he wanted every one of his guests to "feel like a Caesar." That was the old Vegas, the Rat Pack Vegas.

Steve Wynn is generally credited, or blamed, for the "up scaling" of Vegas. Twenty years ago Wynn invented the Vegas of big suites, Dior, Gucci, Chanel, Tiffany, Emeril's, spas and thousand dollar slots. Why rent a room for $40 if you could get somebody to pay

$400 for the same room? Why sell peanuts? Why not sell caviar?

Wynn brought fine art to Vegas: Cézanne, Paul Gauguin, van Gogh, Matisse, Vermeer. A couple of years ago Wynn put his elbow through a $50 million Picasso. No thing. It was all good. He got it fixed.

The new, improved, classy Vegas was a very profitable idea while it lasted. If you owned a casino. Vegas was a magical place where you could put your elbow through your Picasso and still smile, smile, smile. Then President George W. Stupid wrecked Las Vegas along with every other damned thing.

Last year the Vegas economy began to be described with the same mind numbing statistics that are now being used to describe the rest of America. The average room rate in Vegas fell 14 percent. Gambling profits on the strip fell by 26 percent. There are about a thousand of these numbers but you get the idea.

Las Vegas is what you call a "mature market." What that means is that if you are alive and you live on the planet Earth then you probably have already heard about and understand the concept of Las Vegas.

But, people who run businesses never believe that the markets for their product have actually "matured." The people who manufactured personal computers in the 80s or cell phones in the 90s never believed that they might actually run out of new customers some day.

Right now Harley-Davidson, the manufacturer of the most macho of products, is trying to figure out how to sell motorcycles to soccer mommies. Because, you know, there must be just zillions of new customers out there somewhere. The marketing department just hasn't found them yet.

Vegas has had the same reaction. Important people in Vegas are convinced that there must be just zillions of potential visitors out there who have not yet known the joys of big suites, celebrity chefs, big dollar slots and slightly damaged Picassos. There must be some people who have yet to discover that Vegas is all their hopes and dreams made true. Once these people learn of Vegas they will certainly want to travel there and drop a few thousand each and then the city will be saved.

The boss of Vegas these days is a very colorful and charming guy named Oscar Goodman. He is the mayor. He has a colorful past. He used to work in the challenging field of criminal defense. His former clients include Meyer Lansky, Nicky Scarfo, and both "Lefty" Rosenthal and Tony "The Ant" Spilotro.

As a rule of thumb, whether you are a juror or a slot player or a criminal defendant or whatever your problem is, when Oscar Goodman tells you something you believe him. Even if you think Oscar is lying to you, you still believe him. When Oscar says, "Relax. I'm the lawyer. I'll fix it," no matter what your problem may be, you breathe a deep sigh of relief.

So the thing Oscar came up with to fix Vegas was the Vegas Virgins advertising campaign. The premise of this brilliant marketing campaign is very much like the "Whopper Virgins" advertising campaign only better.

In the Whopper Virgins campaign the ad agency sent camera crews out to various Borat and Eskimo countries and introduced all these people in their colorful native costumes to the joys that could be theirs once they just tasted a Double Whopper With Cheese.

"*Ooog glue nick Wooper much we bone,*" some guy in a funny hat would exclaim.

And, a voice-over narrator would translate, "He likes the Whopper With Cheese."

But the Vegas Virgins campaign was different. Way different.

In the Vegas Virgins campaign an ad agency went to a little town in Texas named Cranfills Gap and then flew a third of all the people who lived there out to Vegas for an all expenses paid frolic. The ad agency then filmed all these colorful Texans in their colorful, native Texan costumes enjoying Emeril's and slot machines and the Donnie and Marie show at the Flamingo and all the sights.

"Merle? Can we get front row seats to see comedian of the year Rita Rudner at Harrahs?"

"Hush up! Just hush up now Lulu-Belle! Damnit! I put eight thousand dollars in this here slot so far and I know it is just about to pay off. I can feel it! I can feel it! I'm due! We're gonna be rich Lulu-Belle! We're gone be rich! Here goes!"

See how much better the Vegas campaign is than the Whopper campaign?

No? Well it didn't work anyway. It hasn't worked yet, at least.

Maybe Oscar should have just had George Bush whacked. But he didn't. He tried the Vegas Virgins thing instead. Who are you to judge, anyway? Did you try to have George Bush whacked? Everybody has twenty-twenty hindsight.

On to Plan B. If virgins can't do the trick for Vegas, pardon the expression, maybe whores can.

Prostitution is currently illegal in Las Vegas. Really. Vegas Metro makes about 100 "vice related" arrests on an average weekend.

All of Vegas and Nevada have grown from Mormon roots. So, prostitution is only legal in Nevada in counties that have populations of less than 400,000 people and that vote to allow it. And, the whores are only allowed to do their business in licensed and taxed brothels. Currently there are whorehouses in eight Nevada counties.

And right now, Clark County which surrounds Vegas could not legalize prostitution even if 99 percent of the people voted for it. It is not a "rural county." It has more than 400,000 residents.

Which is a situation that Mayor Goodman thinks should be open for "discussion." Oscar is not actually in favor of legalizing prostitution in Vegas, you understand. He just thinks the subject should be discussed.

And, Goodman has thought the notion should be discussed twice before, in 2004 and 2007. But now, with the financial crisis and all, legalized prostitution in Vegas may be an idea whose time has come. No pun intended.

Oscar told the Las Vegas *Sun* on Thursday that some of his constituents might have "very legitimate" objections to whorehouses. "On the other hand," Goodman mused aloud, "I've met with folks from that industry who make a very compelling argument that it could generate $200 million a year in tax dollars, and that would buy a lot of textbooks, pay for a lot of teachers."

Yes of course! Whores won't just save Goodman's town! They will save the children, too!

If only George W. Bush had grown up in a town with legalized prostitution, he could have gotten a better education and he wouldn't have grown up to be such a moron and Vegas wouldn't be in the mess it is in now! Why can't people ever just do the right thing for the children? They are our future!

And, legalized brothels in Vegas will be good for whores, too. They will save the ladies from "exploiters," which is what Oscar calls the bad pimps. As opposed to the brothel owners who are the good pimps.

Mayor Goodman thinks the good pimps would provide whores with a "sort of an acculturation type of program…where they could get education, they could receive child care instead of leaving their kids in a latchkey situation, classes on self-esteem, those kinds of things."

Oscar is just discussing, you understand. He wants his citizens to be informed.

State Senator Bob Coffin has been listening to Oscar's dispassionate and balanced examination of this issue and he has heard enough. Coffin has decided it is time to open whorehouses in Vegas. "It's almost de facto legal," Coffin said. "It's running unregulated."

"When you're talking about cutting funding for the mentally ill and increasing class sizes for little kids," Coffin continued, "and someone tells me they don't want to tax prostitution, I'm going to call them a hypocrite to their face."

And since we are just discussing, you know. Since we are conversating this issue. wouldn't putting brothels in Las Vegas also solve the problem of all that pesky competition Vegas has been getting from all those Indian casinos?

Why, now that you mention it!

Consider this. They don't have safe, legal, regulated whorehouses in places like Foxwoods or Mohegan Sun or Biloxi now do they? Do they?

Well, if you were an adult entertainment consumer which place would you choose? Would you choose to spend your adult entertainment dollars in a place that cares enough about its children to build them whorehouses? Or would you go to some damn Indian reservation or some damn riverboat that is probably just a breeding ground for the next generation of morons like George W. Bush?

Well isn't the answer obvious?!

And, so may Las Vegas and all its little children and its noble school teachers and its poor bedraggled whores yet be saved. And, live happily ever after.

Chosen Few Week 27

The Federal Case against the Chosen Few Motorcycle Club in Buffalo is now entering its 27th week. The Case began when a 10 page indictment was unsealed last March 17.

But, that indictment was superseded by 30 pages of accusations two weeks later. And, the indictment that superseded that one, on May 19, was 57 pages long. And that second superseding indictment was superseded by yet another 76 pages of accusations two weeks ago.

And, there may be more.

The case began as an investigation into an ongoing dispute between the Chosen Few and two other upstate New York clubs named the Kingsmen and the Lonely Ones. Government prosecutors charged Chosen Few President Alex "Al" Koschtschuk with building five pipe bombs in his garage in the Spring of 2004. A "conspiracy" of six club members including men named Clyde "Butchie" Utz, James "Jimmy" Lathrop, Brion Murphy, Gerald Rogacki and Matthew Watkins then set off one of the bombs to see if it would work.

Then Utz, Murphy and two other desperados named Andy Murray and David Ignasiak threw two of the bombs at the Lonely Ones clubhouse. Koschtschuk told Murray to get rid of the two leftover pipe bombs and five years later, just in time to beat the statute of limitations, the indictment was handed down.

The Chosen Few was founded in Buffalo in 1967. The club wears a Beatnik center patch which symbolizes "freedom and non-conformity with modernistic society." Around Buffalo, the Chosen Few may be most famous for the free concerts they sponsor.

The club has a long and tangled history as a comparatively small club surrounded by larger ones. At one point, the Chosen Few were offered a patch-over by the Hells Angels Motorcycle Club. During another moment in their history about half of the Buffalo Chosen Few joined the American Outlaws Association (AOA.)

The unsealing of the indictment last March culminated a several-months long investigation by the Federal Bureau of Investigation and the Bureau of Alcohol, Tobacco, Firearms and Explosives.

The federal case against the Chosen Few has grown and evolved over the last 27 weeks. Members of the club are now charged with creating a racketeering "enterprise through a pattern of racketeering activity." And, more defendants have been advised of their rights. Names on the indictment now include: Alan Segool, Michael Segool, Bradley Beutler, Dane Beutler, Robert Summerville, Norman Herzog, Robert Treadway, Robert Geiger, Donald Diana, Lionel Carter, Martin Whiteford, Charles Kuznicki, Dennis Rogowski and Gary Phillians.

But, what is truly astounding about this case is that none of the indictments include a single drug charge. The entire case seems to be about the Chosen Few Motorcycle Club pushing its weight around and the Kingsmen Motorcycle Club and the Lonely Ones Motorcycle Club pushing back.

106

Or, as one of the indictments puts it, "Beginning sometime in 2003, the exact date being unknown, the Chosen Few and a rival motorcycle club, the Lonely Ones Motorcycle Club of Blasdell, New York had a dispute which the officers and members of the Chosen Few attempted to win."

- As a result of that dispute the Department of Justice now accuses members of the Chosen Few of: "Representing the local interests of the Outlaws Motorcycle Club by providing an area of operations free from clubs loyal to the Outlaws primary national and international rival, namely the Hells Angels Motorcycle Club by engaging in criminal conduct intended to remove the Lonely Ones Motorcycle Clu, a club loyal to the Hells Angels, from the Western New York area, on behalf of the Outlaws."

- "Making money for the enterprise by running a club which ran a bar and thus sold liquor over the bar from bottles of liquor shipped and transported in interstate and foreign commerce and by sponsoring and charging admission to entertainment events designed to attract members of the public, including members of other motorcycle clubs."

- "Protecting its turf and its reputation from the actions of other motorcycle clubs by committing acts of violence against members and associates of (other) clubs."

- Throwing Molotov Cocktails at the Lonely Ones clubhouse.

- Throwing pipe bombs at the Lonely Ones clubhouse and attempting to murder Lonely Ones patch holder Theodore C. Sparks who was in the clubhouse when members of the Chosen Few threw pipe bombs at it.

- Intentionally damaging "a building located at 100 Main Street, Depew, New York, namely, a vacant house at 100 Main Street by spreading accelerant in the house's interior and lighting it with a time-delayed fuse thus starting a fire causing…damage to the vacant house."
- Stealing a man named Kevin McHenry's motorcycle "by instilling fear in McHenry."
- Stealing $9,300 from a man named Jason Macken "by instilling in Macken fear."
- Stealing a set of mechanic's tools from a man named Matthew Witnauer "by instilling fear in Matthew Witnauer's father, Robert Witnauer, and brother, William Witnauer."
- Trying to shotgun a man named David Carine twice, in December, 2003 and March, 2004.
- Shooting a Kingsmen named William Slater in May, 2005.
- Conspiring to shoot a man named David Ignasiak. Then trying to run over Ignasiak with a pickup truck last April.
- Beating a man named Jason Stucke with baseball bats in October, 2006
- Hitting a Kingsmen patch holder named Eugene Siminski in the back of his head with an axe handle while he was stuck in traffic in August, 2008.
- And, threatening to murder a Kingsmen named David A. Koch.

And, although it is not yet included in a federal indictment a Chosen Few patch holder named Chad Koschuk, who spells his name differently than his father, club president Alex Koschtschuk, was arrested a week ago today on September 14 by the FBI for threatening to sexually assault a male witness in the case.

Assistant U.S. Attorney Anthony Bruce told *The Associated Press* that Koschuk also threatened to cut the witness' hair.

And, Alex Koschtschuk's attorney, Paul Cambria, replied that the government witness started it.

A trial date in this case has not yet been set.

Mark Walker Arrested

Mark Edward "Mean Mark" Walker, 42 and a member of the American Outlaws Association, has been arrested in Ivy Bend, Missouri on a charge of attempted second-degree murder.

Walker was awakened at precisely 6:43 yesterday morning by a total of 26 sworn peace officers comprising: Thirteen members of the Missouri State Water Patrol Special Weapons and Tactics Team; two Deputy United States Marshals; two members of the Mid-Missouri Drug Task Force; eight Morgan County Sheriff's Office Special Weapons and Tactics Team members; and Morgan County Sheriff Jim Petty.

Unsurprisingly, Walker did not attempt to resist. It is still unclear whether or not he was previously aware that he was a wanted man.

According to the police, last July 31st at about 2 a.m., Walker and another member of the Outlaws named Glenn Arthur "Psycho" Sticht, were enjoying some drinks in a bar called the South Pub in Belleview, Florida when they began arguing with a man named Joe Money. Money, 48, was supposedly such an annoyingly skilled and stubborn debater that the two Outlaws were forced to break beer bottles over his head in an attempt to persuade him to concede. Then, allegedly, they started beating him with a pool cue.

During the course of this beating, someone in the bar shot Joe Money in the jaw with a .22-caliber handgun. After conceding the inferiority of his position, Money left the Pub and travelled to the Munroe Regional Medical Center where he sought treatment for the bullet hole in his face. Police found him there.

Police also found the handgun in the bar. Surveillance video led authorities to suspect that Walker and Sticht might have committed a crime.

The next day, police raided the Outlaws Motorcycle Clubhouse at 2140 North Magnolia Avenue in Ocala where they found ammunition and firearms but neither Sticht nor Walker. Sticht was subsequently indicted for aggravated assault. And, when he learned of the charges against him he immediately turned himself in to police in Lakeland, Florida.

Walker meanwhile, eventually relocated to his brother's trailer in Missouri. The elder Walker, Andrew David Walker, 47 has been confined to the Morgan County Detention Center since Valentine's Day on a charge of driving with a revoked license. So it has not yet been determined whether he even knew that his brother had come to town to visit him or not.

The United States Marshal's Florida Regional Fugitive Task Force in Gainesville learned that Andrew David Walker was in jail on the driving charge and suspected that his brother might show up. So, the Marshals asked the Morgan County Sheriff's to investigate.

The Missouri police staked out the trailer, saw Mark Walker enter, called for reinforcements, then waited all night until they were sure that he was asleep before moving in at dawn. "We did confirm that he was at that location yesterday," Sheriff Petty explained. "One of the members of the Water Patrol stayed in the woods all night last night until we executed the search warrant early this morning."

111

Andrew Walker's fiancée, Margaret Berg-Teed was also taken into custody and is being held without bail. The police have not yet decided what charges to bring against her but it is a principal of our system of justice they do not have to show *habeas corpus* until tomorrow.

Ms. Berg-Teed and both Walker brothers are now in the Morgan County Jail.

Myrtle Beach Warns You

The Honorable John Rhodes, Mayor of Myrtle Beach, South Carolina wants you to, "please know that Myrtle Beach is not anti-biker or anti-motorcycle."

Also His Honor wants you to know that if someday you happen to get lost and stray across the frontier from South Carolina into the People's Republic of Myrtle Beach on a perfectly legal motorcycle dressed in a perfectly legal way you will be charged with breaking one of the special Myrtle Beach motorcycle or haberdashery ordinances and have your bike seized.

The Most Excellent and Holy Mayor Rhodes seems to have mastered the most excellent and holy trick of holding two mutually exclusive notions in his head at the same time while believing that both are exclusively true. Maybe it is most excellent that he can do that.

Maybe the simple fact is that Myrtle Beach has just formally declared war on bikers -on a website you can visit at www.myrtlebeachbikerinfo.com.

"Myrtle Beach is no longer the location for two long-running motorcycle events," the mayor decrees on the site. The events which the mayor cannot bring himself to name are the Harley-Davidson Dealers Association Spring Rally and the Atlantic Beach

Memorial Day Bikefest. "After many years, our residents grew weary of three weeks of noise and traffic congestion each May," the mayor continues, "and they asked City Council to end the events."

The method the city has chosen to "end the events" is zero tolerance for violators of fifteen or so brand new laws. The most draconian of these pertain to the noise you make, the way you dress and where you stand.

The mayor explains the noise ordinance as "No loud mufflers. No straight pipes." Which is, of course, a flat out lie. "Loud" means louder than 83 decibels which is much quieter than almost any public place. And, the consequences of having a cop, who may or not know how to use a decibel meter, determining that your motorcycle is "loud" is the seizure of your bike. You cannot just say, "Sorry, officer. I was looking for South Carolina and got lost." They take your bike.

The haberdashery ordinance is the Myrtle Beach helmet law. Without an "approved" helmet you cannot ride a motorcycle in the city. And, as with the noise regulation, if you cannot ride you cannot leave. At least not with your bike.

And, there are several "loitering" ordinances. What they all say is that if you are taking up space in a parking lot or on a sidewalk or if you are standing in a store and you do not have money in your hand you are breaking the law.

A city spokesman named Mark Kruea elaborated, "We have new laws, and we would rather not surprise visitors. We would rather they have some idea of what to expect when they come here." Sure thing, Boss Kruea.

Of course, neither Warden Rhodes nor Boss Kruea nor the Myrtle Beach guards have yet managed the miracle of omnipotence. So, technically, you can stand one foot across the free side of the Myrtle Beach

De-Militarized Zone and still be your loud, rude, socially unacceptable self.

Just make sure you know the exact location of that line. And, if you do happen to find yourself in Myrtle Beach you should expect to be bullied.

Myrtle Beach Laugh Riot

Myrtle Beach Bike Week is turning to slapstick. If you actually are in the greater North Carolina-South Carolina metropolitan area this May expect to see Keystone Kops, clowns throwing pies and Mel Brooks and Albert Brooks and Woody Allen all zooming up and down the coast in camera trucks.

First, you know about the new Myrtle Beach laws. Right? The city of Myrtle Beach has passed a set of laws designed to seize your motorcycle, drive you out of town on foot and encourage, "Y'all, to don't be stupid now and try to come back. Boy. Y'all come back we gone make y'all squeal like a pig. Soo-wee!"

In all of South Carolina, only Myrtle Beach has a helmet law. And a hundred, idealistic, American bikers, brave sons of both the North and the South challenged that law last weekend. Fifty-seven of them won themselves $100 tickets. Five got warnings. One was ticketed for parking his bike in the wrong place.

Horry County does not want you. Atlantic Beach does not want you. Maybe North Myrtle Beach still wants you but the rest of Horry County is working on them and there are still ten weeks to go.

So who wants you? Myrtle Beach Harley-Davidson wants you. That is who. They want you a whole lot.

Mike Shank, who seems to speak for both Festival Productions and the local Harley dealership continues to try with all his might to paint a big, old, bright smiley face on this heaping pile of Mongolian cluster love. The Festival Productions rally – call it "Cruising the Coast" and don't even bring up the subject of names – is still scheduled to blast off May 8th and linger until May 17th.

That is if, and right now it is a very big if, Myrtle Beach does not manage to get its hands on its very own nuclear bomb between now and then.

Just a little well-meaning advice here, okay? If you are down there this May and you happen to actually be able to see the city of Myrtle Beach through binoculars or a telescope or a long camera lens or whatever you got? And, you notice that the good citizens of Myrtle Beach are putting on, like, dark glasses and radiation suits? You might consider trying to run.

Meanwhile, the Carolina Harley-Davidson Dealers Association, has announced that it is moving its annual Spring Rally all the way out of South Carolina. This year's official Harley rally will be held in New Bern, North Carolina on May 15th and 16th.

New Bern is the second oldest town in North Carolina. They have hotels and a waterfront and they are only about 20 miles from the nearest beach. This rally will be held at the fairgrounds just outside of town.

And, they just love them some tourists down there in New Bern, North Carolina. Whoo boy! You know, what with the economy killing everybody's vacation and all? Tourist business is in the toilet, partner.

So, they would just love for you to come on down. Hell, they are practically right up on the South of the Border motel, truck stop, souvenir emporium and fire works stand. If you have never been there you have to go. Forget Paris, France. You have to see the South of the Border at least once. Pedro says so.

Mayor T.A. Bayliss III, issued a press release in which he sincerely stated that New Bern is, "pleased and honored...to hold your rally in our city, and we pledge our total cooperation in making your rally a most pleasurable and memorable occasion for all in attendance."

Of course, Mayor Bayliss is under the impression that only about 4,000 "older people" are going to show up for this thing. When *The Associated Press* asked him about the possibility that a hundred thousand or so bikers might soon be on their way, His Honor was shocked! Shocked!

"Absolutely not," he said. "We couldn't handle it. There's no way in the world."

Prep the whipped cream pies. Standby the Keystone Kops. Send in the clowns. Everybody, now y'all have fun. Ya' hear?

Tweeting The Incarceration Experience

First Steven Spielberg showed all the rest of us "what war is really like."

Spielberg, who spent the fairly ferocious year 1968 making a film called *Amblin'* for Universal Studios, has frankly explained, "My immediate political activity (at the height of the Vietnam War) was based on self-preservation. I had a draft counselor. I legally did what I could to not go." But Spielberg reckoned his vision of war to be true because, "Vietnam pushed people from my generation to tell the truth about war without glorifying it."

Then, in case you hadn't heard, another artist named Kurt Sutter has created an "adrenalized drama with darkly comedic undertones that explores a notorious outlaw motorcycle club's desire to protect its livelihood while ensuring that their simple, sheltered town of Charming, California remains exactly that, Charming." The drama is a television show called *Sons of Anarchy* – in case the promotional copy left you confused – and after Sutter actually learned to ride a motorcycle, critics agreed, the show kicked "into a second gear!"

Finally, last Thursday Academy Award winning screenwriter and auteur Roger Avary was handed the opportunity to dial his jail stories up a notch. Avary has about seven months left on a one minute bit (good time makes it eight months) in the Ventura County Jail.

For the last month Avary, calling himself #34, has been tweeting about his exciting adventures in that sordid, mundane place to 9,538 rapt followers.

"Sickness spreads throughout the facility like brush fires, and #34 is helpless to avoid the outbreak and inevitable infection," Avary tweeted November 22. The day before that he tweeted, "A ball of Heroin tar is found on an inmate. The guards react lightning-fast, locking down the facility and 'rolling up' those responsible."

Two weeks earlier Avary tweeted, "It's your birthday! announcing that #34 is to receive a random strip-down and cavity search to be performed by a leering, rotund officer." Last Tuesday Avary announced, "#34's new roomie, EZ, takes Yeyo's old bunk, locker, AND number. He regales awesome tales about his former life as an Oxnard gangbanger."

Yeyo? Like slang for old school back in the day? Anyway, *The Aging Rebel* has not been able to confirm whether Steven Spielberg or Kurt Sutter are among Avary's thousands of followers. Fox Searchlight, however, a division of Fox Studios has been following Avary's tweets.

And comic book author, Neil Gaiman – who the *Dictionary of Literary Biography* lists as one of the top ten, living, postmodern writers – is enthralled by Avary's accounts of life inside. "My friend @AVARY is tweeting from the inside. It's riveting, horrible strange," Gaiman himself tweeted. "Jail in 140 character lumps."

Avary is a short, round and self-important man who co-wrote the screenplays for *Pulp Fiction* and *Reservoir Dogs*. He also produced, wrote and directed

Rules of Attraction, *Glitterati* and the animated *Beowulf*. He is currently working on *Return to Castle Wolfenstein*.

Avary was sentenced to jail and five years probation for a drunken driving accident that went bad in January 2008 in Ojai, California. Avary was drunk and hit a tree. His wife Gretchen was seriously injured. An Italian fan name Andreas Zini was killed.

Zini and his new wife were in Los Angeles on their honeymoon. Zini was a big fan of *Pulp Fiction* so he contacted Avary and offered to buy him dinner. It was the only time the two men ever met.

Avary faced up to eleven years in prison but because he had no criminal history and because of his "standing in the community" he was sentenced to a minimum term in County Jail. Public records indicate Avary actually spent eleven minutes in jail on October 26 and then was assigned to a work furlough program. He spent nights and weekends in a low security barracks at the Camarillo Airport. He was released everyday to go to a production office to work on *Return to Castle Wolfenstein*.

The tweets were sent from a computer at the production office. Last week the Ventura County Sheriff learned about Avary's masquerade and ordered that he do his time in the actual jail – at least until the bad publicity goes away.

""#34 is 'rolled up' to a higher security facility for exercising his first amendment rights," Avary tweeted Thanksgiving night. "The truth he has discovered is too dangerous."

Or maybe Roger was just really stupid. But there is a bright side to this unfortunate series of events. Now Avary has a chance to really know what jail is really like. "Hey Roger? Roger? Yo? Roger! Roger! Are you that guy? Are you that *Pulp Fiction* guy? I thought his name was Tarantino? Are you rich? You gonna eat that? Are you sure? Can I have your bread?"

121

Stahlman Trial Begins

All the little tragedies climax in either an operating room, a courtroom or a morgue. The little tragedy of one-time Outlaws Motorcycle Club member Ronald Stahlman has found its moment in an old, stone courthouse in Warren, Ohio.

On April 28, 1979, Stahlman went out drinking in Warren with friends. One of the friends, Roger Collins, was driving Stahlman home in his pickup truck when he rear-ended a car driven by 18-year-old Bernard Williamson. It was 3:30 on the morning of the 29th.

Williamson jumped out of his car and wanted to fight. Williamson's passenger, a woman named Debbie Bush went to a phone booth to call police. Two witnesses, Glen Ellison and Patricia Strickland, remember that 29 years ago in the middle of the night Williamson was beating Collins and Stahlman got out of the truck to help him.

When the police arrived they found that Williamson had been stabbed nine times. He died in the street.

There is no physical evidence in the case. There is no murder weapon. The police who investigated the killing are dead or unable to testify. Some of the crime scene photographs have disappeared. All that is left is the tragedy.

According to prosecutors, after the fight Collins and Stahlman went to Collins' house in Lordstown, Ohio. Then they went to Franklin, Pennsylvania for a week. Then Stahlman went home and together with his wife Pam and his two small daughters Tina and Rhonda, Stahlman left town.

About the time Stahlman was moving out Collins turned himself in and confessed. He confessed that Stahlman had stabbed Williamson. He pled guilty to assault and obstruction of justice and he paid his debt to society with a six month stretch in the Trumbull County jail.

Yesterday Collins testified that he was not even awake when Williamson was stabbed. "I got knocked down pretty quick. I think I was out, too, for a moment." The next thing Collins knew, he had a cut on his arm and Williamson was "sitting there, leaning on the car, so I ran past him and got into the (truck) cab."

Then according to Collins, Stahlman confessed what he had done. "We were going down the road. Ron was kind of upset. He says, 'I think I might have stabbed that guy,'" Collins told the court.

Stahlman changed his name to Jim O'Neil. His wife went by her maiden name Pam Liebal. They started a new, good life in a little town named Payson, off the beaten track, in the high pine country halfway between Mesa and Winslow, Arizona. The little girls grew up. The case went cold. The tragic past became a bad dream.

In 1993, before anybody paid much attention to the internet, Jim O'Neil and Pam Liebal had the names on their daughters' social security cards legally changed to O'Neil. And, fifteen years later that is how tragedy found them.

The Warren police had so little crime in 2005 that a detective named Brian Holmes was told to work cold cases. He reopened the Williamson case and convinced a U.S. Marshall with Warren ties, named Bill Bolden, to work the case with him. Still another police force, this one called the Northern Ohio Violent Fugitive Task Force, was enlisted in the search for Stahlman.

A snitch told the cold case cops that Stahlman had moved to Phoenix so Holmes and Bolden began to look for him on the internet. Late last year the two discovered that Tina and Rhonda Stahlman, residing in Payson, Arizona had legally changed their names to Tina and Rhonda O'Neil. After that it was easy.

Ron Stahlman was quickly arrested, extradited back to Ohio and he has been a prisoner ever since. He was been locked up in the same jail for almost as long as his old friend Roger Collins who is now the chief witness against him.

The prosecution is expected to conclude its case tomorrow. Arguments may be heard as early as Friday. The jury may return a verdict as early as then. And then this particular little tragedy may conclude or maybe it will not.

Maybe Jim O'Neil can return to his life up on the Mogollon Rim or maybe the man he used to be, Ron Stahlman, will never spend another night with his wife again. Maybe it will finally be finished or maybe it is over.

Yesterday the court made Ron Stahlman watch as the prosecution put his wife and his daughters and his mother on the stand. Stahlman had to watch while the man who was once his best friend tried to put him in prison.

And for all of this, Bernard Williamson, who died in a street in Warren, Ohio 29 years ago, is still dead.

Hugh Harrison "Harry" Hurt

Harry Hurt, the author of the only comprehensive investigation ever made into the factors that effect motorcycle safety, died November 29th at Pomona Valley Hospital east of Los Angeles. Susan Carpenter of the Los Angeles *Times* has reported that he died from a heart attack that was the result of back surgery on November 22nd.

Hurt's first motorcycle was a Cushman scooter he tore apart and rebuilt as a kid in Big Springs, Texas. He graduated from Texas A&M in 1950 and served as a Navy pilot in Korea. After his discharge, he rode from Texas to California on a 1947, EL 61 Knucklehead. He earned a Master's degree in Engineering at the University of Southern California and joined the faculty there. His advisor and mentor was Charles "Red" Lombard who invented and patented the energy-absorbing motorcycle helmet in 1953.

Hurt was working at the USC Traffic Safety Center in 1975 when the National Highway Traffic Safety Administration asked him to do a scientific study of motorcycle injuries and crashes. During 1976 and 1977 Hurt and two other USC researches named David Thom and James Ouellet conducted on-scene investigations of 900 motorcycle accidents in Los

Angeles County. The researchers photographed, examined and measured each accident site; interviewed the survivors; interviewed 2,310 passing motorcyclists; and studied 3,600 police reports of other accidents reported at those sites.

In 1981 Hurt published a book titled, *Volume I: Technical Report, Motorcycle Accident Cause Factors and Identification of Countermeasures, January, 1981 - Final Report*. Nobody wanted to have to say all that, however, so for the last 38 years it has simply been called *The Hurt Report*.

What Hurt concluded never surprised motorcyclists and his long held prejudice in favor of helmet laws still infuriated some bikers until his dying day.

In 1981, Hurt assumed that his would be only the first of many studies into motorcycle safety. As it turned out *The Hurt Report* was the one and only. And, his results were skewed by the time and place, Los Angeles in the late seventies, where his study was conducted. So, for example, a similar study conducted in some other place would indicate far more accidents caused by collisions with deer, wild turkeys and feral pigs. And, in 1977 the phrase "road rage" had not yet been coined.

The official summary of Hurt's findings supplied by the National Technical Information Service includes the following conclusions.

- Approximately three-fourths of motorcycle accidents involved collision with another vehicle, which was most often a passenger automobile.
- Approximately one-fourth of motorcycle accidents were single vehicle accidents involving the motorcycle colliding with the roadway or some fixed object in the environment.

- Vehicle failure accounted for less than three percent of motorcycle accidents, and most of those are single vehicle accidents where control was lost due to a puncture flat.
- In single vehicle accidents, motorcycle rider error was present as the accident precipitating factor in about two-thirds of the cases, with the typical error being a slide-out and fall due to over-braking or running wide on a curve due to excess speed or under-cornering.
- Roadway defects (pavement ridges, potholes, etc.) were the accident cause in two percent of the accidents; animal involvement was one percent of the accidents.
- In multiple vehicle accidents, the driver of the other vehicle violated the motorcycle right-of-way and caused the accident two-thirds of the time.
- The failure of motorists to detect and recognize motorcycles in traffic is the predominating cause of motorcycle accidents. The driver of the other vehicle involved in collision with the motorcycle did not see the motorcycle before the collision, or did not see the motorcycle until too late to avoid the collision.
- Deliberate hostile action by a motorist against a motorcycle rider is a rare accident cause. The most frequent accident configuration is the motorcycle proceeding straight then the automobile makes a left turn in front of the oncoming motorcycle.
- Intersections are the most likely place for the motorcycle accident, with the other vehicle violating the motorcycle right of-way, and often violating traffic controls.

- Weather is not a factor in ninety-eight percent of motorcycle accidents.
- Most motorcycle accidents involve a short trip associated with shopping, errands, friends, entertainment or recreation, and the accident is likely to happen in a very short time close to the trip origin.
- The view of the motorcycle or the other vehicle involved in the accident is limited by glare or obstructed by other vehicles in almost half of the multiple vehicle accidents.
- Conspicuity of the motorcycle is a critical factor in the multiple vehicle accidents, and accident involvement is significantly reduced by the use of motorcycle headlamps (on in daylight) and the wearing of high visibility yellow, orange or bright red jackets.
- Fuel system leaks and spills were present in 62% of the motorcycle accidents in the post-crash phase. This represents an undue hazard for fire.
- The median pre-crash speed was 29.8 mph, and the median crash speed was 21.5 mph, and the one-in-a-thousand crash speed is approximately 86 mph.
- The typical motorcycle pre-crash lines-of-sight to the traffic hazard portray no contribution of the limits of peripheral vision; more than three-fourths of all accident hazards are within forty-five degrees of either side of straight ahead.
- Conspicuity of the motorcycle is most critical for the frontal surfaces of the motorcycle and rider.
- Vehicle defects related to accident causation are rare and likely to be due to deficient or defective maintenance.

- Motorcycle riders between the ages of 16 and 24 are significantly overrepresented in accidents; motorcycle riders between the ages of 30 and 50 are significantly underrepresented. Although the majority of the accident-involved motorcycle riders are male (ninety-six percent,) the female motorcycles riders are significantly overrepresented in the accident data.
- Craftsmen, laborers, and students comprise most of the accident-involved motorcycle riders. Professionals, sales workers, and craftsmen are underrepresented and laborers, students and unemployed are overrepresented in the accidents.
- Motorcycle riders with previous recent traffic citations and accidents are overrepresented in the accident data.
- The motorcycle riders involved in accidents are essentially without training; ninety-two percent were self-taught or learned from family or friends. Motorcycle rider training experience reduces accident involvement and is related to reduced injuries in the event of accidents.
- More than half of the accident-involved motorcycle riders had less than five months experience on the accident motorcycle, although the total street riding experience was almost three years. Motorcycle riders with dirt bike experience are significantly underrepresented in the accident data.

Lack of attention to the driving task is a common factor for the motorcyclist in an accident.

- Almost half of the fatal accidents show alcohol involvement.
- Motorcycle riders in these accidents showed significant collision avoidance problems. Most

riders would over-brake and skid the rear wheel, and under-brake the front wheel greatly reducing collision avoidance deceleration. The ability to countersteer and swerve was essentially absent.

- The typical motorcycle accident allows the motorcyclist just less than 2 seconds to complete all collision avoidance action.

- Passenger-carrying motorcycles are not overrepresented in the accident area.

- The driver of the other vehicles involved in collision with the motorcycle are not distinguished from other accident populations except that the ages of 20 to 29, and beyond 65 are overrepresented. Also, these drivers are generally unfamiliar with motorcycles.

- Large displacement motorcycles are underrepresented in accidents but they are associated with higher injury severity when involved in accidents.

- Any effect of motorcycle color on accident involvement is not determinable from these data, but is expected to be insignificant because the frontal surfaces are most often presented to the other vehicle involved in the collision.

- Motorcycles equipped with fairings and windshields are underrepresented in accidents, most likely because of the contribution to conspicuity and the association with more experienced and trained riders.

- Motorcycle riders in these accidents were significantly without motorcycle license, without any license, or with license revoked.

- Motorcycle modifications such as those associated with the semi-chopper or cafe racer are definitely overrepresented in accidents.

- The likelihood of injury is extremely high in these motorcycle accidents. Ninety-eight percent of the multiple vehicle collisions and ninety-six percent of the single vehicle accidents resulted in some kind of injury to the motorcycle rider. Forty-five percent resulted in more than a minor injury.
- Half of the injuries to the somatic regions were to the ankle-foot, lower leg, knee, and thigh-upper leg.
- Crash bars are not an effective injury countermeasure; the reduction of injury to the ankle-foot is balanced by increase of injury to the thigh-upper leg, knee, and lower leg.
- The use of heavy boots, jacket, gloves, etc., is effective in preventing or reducing abrasions and lacerations, which are frequent but rarely severe injuries.
- Groin injuries were sustained by the motorcyclist in at least 13% of the accidents, which typified by multiple vehicle collision in frontal impact at higher than average speed.
- Injury severity increases with speed, alcohol involvement and motorcycle size.
- Seventy-three percent of the accident-involved motorcycle riders used no eye protection, and it is likely that the wind on the unprotected eyes contributed in impairment of vision which delayed hazard detection.

In 1990, *Motorcyclist* magazine named Hurt "Motorcyclist of the Decade."

Hurt is survived by his widow, Joan; his sons Harry and John; his daughters Julie, Vivien and Vera; and ten grandchildren.

Harry Hurt was 81. He tried to help.

Railroad Tie Kills Rider

Road debris killed another biker last week.

Carl Pierson, a member of an informal motorcycle club called the "Lake Pirates," was killed and three others were injured after the lead two bikes in a small pack hit a railroad tie. The collision happened on a service road of US Route 75 in McKinney, Texas.

"All of a sudden I just saw smoke, motorcycles colliding and they started flying" George Henley told television station *WFAA* in Dallas. Henley was riding in the back of the pack. He told the station he escaped serious injury when he threw his "motorcycle to the side."

The standard dimensions of a railroad tie are 9" X 7" X 102". Harley-Davidson motorcycles generally ride about five inches off the ground.

Besides supporting railroad tracks, wooden railroad ties are typically sold in home improvement stores and used in landscaping. Some ties are cut and designed specifically for that purpose. The tie involved in the Texas accident was clearly a used railroad tie. These used ties are cheaper than "landscaping ties" and weigh about 200 pounds. The accident scene is within sight of a Home Depot.

Henley told the Dallas television station that he believed the debris had been intentionally placed in the road as a prank and was not an accident. "I know it's intentional," he said. "It was completely horizontal on the road, and it was in a very dark spot."

The Lake Pirates are offering a $3,000 reward to anyone who can explain how the railroad tie wound up in the road. One place to look might be the sales records of the Home Depot near the accident.

All bikers know how dangerous road debris can be. Studies of the problem are few and far between. The last time the hazard was newsworthy was in 2007 when the New York *Times* ran a 1300 word, tongue-in-cheek feature on the subject.

The British Motorcyclists Federation estimated that 6 percent of all motorcycle accidents in Britain in 2005 were caused by road debris. The Ohio State Patrol estimated that 13 percent of all debris related crashes from 2004 to 2006 involved motorcycles. The AAA Foundation for Traffic Safety estimated in 2004 that road debris causes about 80 deaths in the United States each year.

However, AAA may have significantly underestimated the actual hazard.

In California alone, 155 people were killed in accidents caused by road debris in 2005 and 2006. In 2006 the California Department of Transportation (CALTRANS) removed 140,000 cubic yards of debris from the freeways. That volume would fill about 9,000 dump trucks.

Most debris on the California freeways is what CALTRANS calls "unintentional litter." Typically, unintentional litter is unsecured cargo like railroad ties, mattresses, stoves and refrigerators that fly off the backs of pickup trucks and the roofs of automobiles.

One of the few states that has tried to do something about the problem is Washington. In 2005,

Washington passed "Maria's Law." The law is named for a woman who was blinded when a wooden shelf flew off a trailer and smashed through her windshield. Maria's Law raised the penalty for carrying an unsecured load from $194 to a maximum of $5000 and a year in jail.

Carl Pierson was engaged and he was the father of a 13-year-old daughter.

Tommy "Tommy Gun" Martinez

Tommy "Tommy Gun" Martinez died December 24, 2009. He was a patch holder in the American Latino Motorcycle Association. A.L.M.A. is a one piece patch club in Phoenix and the club lost two brothers in less than two weeks.

Max Joseph "Dragon" Aragon died January 3 as he was returning home from Martinez' wake.

Martinez was a founding member of A.L.M.A. and the club's road captain. He was the first member of the club to die.

Tommy Gun Martinez is survived by his wife Becky, his sons Tommy and Ricky, his daughter-in-law Yvonne, his three grandchildren Victoria, Isaiah and Noah, his friend Dru and his club brothers.

He was a friend. He died happy.

Requiescat In Pace

Max Joseph Aragon

Max Joseph "Dragon" Aragon died January 3 and he was buried last Saturday at Greenwood Memory Lawn Cemetery in Phoenix. He was a patch holder in the American Latino Motorcycle Association. A.L.M.A. is a one piece patch club in Phoenix and a member of the Arizona Confederation of Clubs.

Max Aragon was riding his motorcycle on the Thomas Road off ramp from Grand Avenue in Phoenix about 1:30 am two days into the new year when he had a terrible accident. A Phoenix police spokesman named James Holmes speculated that Aragon hit a cement wall and fell off his bike. Holmes also guessed that the bike kept going for another 150 yards.

Police responded to a report of the accident and impounded the bike about 2 am but never looked for Aragon. "First of all, you have a huge area on Grand Avenue with all the overpasses," Police Lieutenant Michael Rivera told *KNXV* in Phoenix. "It's dark. It may appear obvious to us, but when someone recovers a bike it could be anything. A hit and run...a stolen bike."

A vagrant found Aragon's body about noon the next day.

Aragon is survived by his wife Irma; his sons Joseph and Tony; his father Max; his mother Bea and his brothers in the American Latino Motorcycle Association.

Max Dragon Aragon was 41-years-old. He was a friend and he will be missed. He died with his boots on.

James Alan "Wolf" Corrao

James Wolf Corrao died at dusk on March 16when his motorcycle was struck by a 1999 Dodge pickup truck at the corner of Tropicana Avenue and Titanium Avenue in Las Vegas, Nevada.

Carrao's wife Debbie was following her husband on another motorcycle and was injured when she had to put her bike down on the low side to avoid the truck.

The pickup was being driven by Carlow Henriquez, 52, of Las Vegas. Henriquez fled the scene of the accident and was apprehended a block away after he crashed into a fence. Henriquez was arrested for felony drunk driving, felony hit and run, unsafe lane change and driving with an open container of an alcoholic beverage.

Both James and Debbie Corrao were transported to Sunrise Hospital where he was pronounced dead.

James Wolf Corrao was a long-time and enormously respected member of the Soldiers for Jesus Motorcycle Club. Before he found the Lord, Wolf Corrao had been a member in good standing of another major motorcycle club. His funeral last Saturday was attended by 600 mourners. And, the respect with which he was regarded is evidenced by the attendance of members of the Vagos Motorcycle Club, the Hells Angels Motorcycle Club and the Bandidos Motorcycle Club.

He was born in Cleveland, Ohio and moved to Las Vegas in 1982.

He is survived by his widow; his daughters Angie and Jamie; his sons Jesse James and William Cody; six grandchildren; three sisters; four brothers; his brother Soldiers for Jesus; and many hundreds of brothers in the wind.

James Alan Wolf Corrao was 53-years-old. He died with his boots on.

Requiescat In Pace

Property Of John

Sarah Palin, John McCain and the celebrity bike builder Paul Teutel all converged in suburban Philadelphia yesterday, as the Wild Ones once converged on Hollister.

Ms. Palin, who may soon be a heartbeat from the Presidency, wore a red leather jacket to introduce Teutel on the steps of the courthouse in Media, PA. The multi-millionaire Teutel, who plays a grumpy and opinionated biker on reality TV, then rode one of his motorcycles up a ramp and onto a stage.

He was accompanied by his sons, Paul Jr. and Mikey. Heavy metal music boomed from loudspeakers. And, as he took the microphone from Ms. Palin, the music faded and everyone cheered.

"How many people out there love their country and the military," Teutel asked. There was general agreement that everyone loved America although Teutel neglected to raise the question of what everybody means by that. He also inferred that everyone loves the military and left alone the question of how most Americans feel about the military when it actually involves the enlistment of their own sons.

Neither Paul Jr. nor Mikey revealed their plans to serve, or if to serve when, in which branch or for how long.

Then referring to John McCain's heroic service and the years during which he was tortured by the North Vietnamese, Teutel said his bike "represents that." It represents, "All the people who have been POW-MIA. This bike represents that."

"Marvelous," McCain replied when it was his turn to hold the microphone. "Sarah and I are going to get on that chopper and ride it right to Washington and raise hell when we get there." It was a fairly orchestrated event so McCain did not elaborate.

Nevertheless, bikers may continue to fantasize and hope that if only enough of them vote for McCain and Ms. Palin, they may someday be rewarded with a glimpse of the Alaska governor enthusiastically participating in one of the traditional biker field events. Like, oh, say, the weenie bite.

Ms. Palin continues to be the star of Senator McCain's campaign. She is photogenic and seems good natured. She also seems to be almost supernaturally vice free and also appears to have virtually no public record for anyone to criticize.

Yesterday on the courthouse steps in Media, people chanted even more loudly for her than they did for the motorcycle and she spoke for almost as long as her running mate.

Former President Bill Clinton meeting the press in New York, was quoted as saying he understands why she is so popular.

"I come from Arkansas," Clinton said. "I get why she's hot."

Obama Snubs Rolling Thunder

President Barack Obama almost snubbed Rolling Thunder Friday. Then at the last minute he changed his mind. Or, maybe his basketball game ended early.

About 3:30 in the afternoon, "The president stopped by while members of Rolling Thunder were meeting with administration officials about veterans' issues," Nick Shapiro, a propagandist with the Ministry of Truth, told the White House press pool. "He was very happy to meet with them." Shapiro described the meeting as "brief but cordial."

Shapiro was unable to say if the President was as happy to meet the veterans as he has said he would be to meet with the President of Iran. Given the spontaneity of the meeting, one would guess not so much.

As recently as May 15, the White House was refusing to even acknowledge Rolling Thunder. Then the President agreed to allow an official to accept a letter from the group. Friday morning, the situation had evolved a little more and the White House announced that unnamed "officials" had agreed to actually "meet" with representatives of Rolling Thunder. Then, at the last minute, the big boss himself dropped in.

Whine if you must about losing your job and your house and your wife and your dog, the respect given to veterans was very much greater under the tyranny of George W. Bush. That is unless you are talking about veteran's benefits or something tangible like that. But symbolically, veterans were much more important to Bush than they are to Obama.

Last year representatives of Rolling Thunder gave the President an official Rolling Thunder cut. The former President smirked and pulled on the garment and either he tried to dance or he tried to walk. With that guy who could tell? Whatever it was, he definitely did not throw his leg over a motorcycle. But, he smirked very respectfully.

Saturday morning the Washington *Post* reported that the cooler reception given to Rolling Thunder this year showed "The culture of the White House appear(s) to have changed."

Whether the cultural change on Pennsylvania Avenue is proper or rude has not yet been brought up for debate and probably will never will be. On the other hand, it is a stark fact that Rolling Thunder has always been a demonstration by one side in the culture war for America's hearts and minds. And, it is an equally stark fact that the culture war seems destined to never, ever end.

In the distant, pre-*Eyewitless News* past, Rolling Thunder was first a bombing campaign, then a rock concert tour, then a slogan on a Harley tee shirt. The motorcycle ride of that name was invented by three Vietnam Veterans named Ray Manzo, John Holland and Walt Sides in 1987. The three decided to start an annual ride to the Vietnam Veterans Memorial in

Washington. And, it is probably fair to say their intentions were at least aggressive.

The Memorial, which most people just call The Wall, opened in 1982 and five years later it was still controversial. The majority opinion, clearly, was that nothing connected to Vietnam should ever be memorialized. A large, opposing group argued that The Wall was hardly a monument at all. About 1987, a number of Veterans began to believe that even if The Wall was not much it was still ours.

Some of those veterans had come home and become outlaws. Rolling Thunder first gained national attention in 1988 after Manzo, Holland, Sides and a man named Artie Muller enlisted the help of the Vietnam Veterans (VNV) Motorcycle Club.

That year, and to a lesser extent today, this event had two parts.

The first and, for most participants, the most important component was "The Run To The Wall." Near the end of the Cosby years, The Run To The Wall was an almost holy, cross-continental pilgrimage that began at the TA Truck Stop in Ontario, California. Those first years, fifty or so underemployed, allegedly criminal, Vietnam Vets would wind themselves up and charge like berserkers from one ocean to the other.

The Run was such an audacious idea that it picked up riders as it moved east—like the Lord rounding up disciples on the shores of the Galilee. Good citizens were so astounded by this pilgrimage that some applauded the pack. Cops stopped traffic to let the veterans pass. Cops! Bike shops offered free oil changes. Very quickly, The Run To The Wall became a welcome home parade.

The second part of the event was called Rolling Thunder. Riders from the west, south, north and east would assemble in Virginia and ride as one huge pack to The Wall. In 1988, 2,000 Vietnam Vets and their supporters and survivors rode in that pack.

Rolling Thunder in 1988 was a *de facto* outlaw event so, of course, there were arrests. Most veterans that year were concerned about the men who were still missing fifteen years after the end of the war. So, naturally several biker criminals ran onto the grass behind The Wall, waved POW-MIA flags, were cheered by the assembled crowd and then were dragged away by U.S. Park Police for demonstrating without a permit. After that, other than a couple of joints, everybody behaved.

Eighty-eight was a year when it was still acceptable to stereotype Vietnam Veterans as beasts. The Wall was vandalized that spring. Someone tried to scratch out the names on three of the panels but The Wall is granite, the "protest" was furtive and the monument was roughed up not maimed.

No sitting politician dared attend or even acknowledge the event but a former Senator named Charles Mathias did speak and he apologized to the group for the recent vandalization. Mathias called the vandals "utterly without thought."

In 1988, it was still considered absolutely necessary that Vietnam Veterans apologize for "what they had done." So when a Vietnam Veteran named Marshall Colt spoke he began his remarks very humbly.

"I would like to thank our nation for gradually accepting Vietnam Veterans and separating the war from the warriors and recognizing that Vietnam Veterans honored a commitment to the country," Colt said. Then, because America never would, Colt took it upon himself to forgive the mostly rough crowd for its sins. " I am proud of the honorable intentions of you, my compatriots," he said.

Colt's remarks were intended kindly, of course. All the speakers were trying to be nice. A woman named Laura Palmer stood up and said, "Welcome home."

But, many of the men in the crowd had a different idea of what was going on that day. A biker from Pittsburgh named Robert Wagner called the rally by The Wall, "a show of strength." Really, it was just a little rally by the unpopular side in the culture war.

Music from an improvised sound system drifted out over the lawn, where it roused an army of tiny insects. The insects made their own show of strength, sought their respect, then retreated to the Reflecting Pool.

Many bikers lingered, searched, sought names lost in a jungle of names, gave up and made their own retreat. It was all mostly over in about ninety minutes. It was not much of a payoff after such a long, hard ride.

But Rolling Thunder did not die. It changed with the times.

Eric Hoffer, the self-taught, stevedore philosopher noticed that "Every good idea in America ends up as a corporation, a foundation or a racket." And, so Rolling Thunder is now incorporated.

Rolling Thunder has become the great thing Artie Muller has done with his life. Muller was a sergeant in the Fourth Infantry Division in the Central Highlands. He has been widely described by friends and enemies as "charismatic." He soon separated the VNVMC from the run and the parade and after he did Rolling Thunder seemed to become more respectable.

Rolling Thunder became less an outlaw "show of force" and more a chance to "honor the vets." It grew to 40,000 riders by 1994. Last year 350,000 riders took part.

Rolling Thunder, Incorporated is now a quasi-motorcycle club with 88 chapters in 29 states. The phrases Rolling Thunder and Rolling Thunder Charities are registered trademarks. And, the organization's web site warns visitors that: "Use of these trademarks or any combination thereafter of said trademarks by any outside entity, is strictly prohibited. Failure to comply with the Trademark laws will result in legal action against any person/s and or business interest using said trademarks."

Rolling Thunder is Artie Muller's club. He has sincerely and whole-heartedly advocated for veterans for most of his life. He handed Bush his Rolling Thunder cut last year and it was Artie Muller who Obama decided not to snub on Friday. Muller gets his respect on behalf of the vets.

Yet, as Rolling Thunder has grown gargantuan the other side in the culture war has more aggressively tried to belittle the veterans' parade. For the last year, the foremost advocate for shoving the vets back into their tiger cages has been Garrison Keillor.

Keillor is, as part of his official job description, America's most beloved humorist. And, in case no one has ever explained it to you, a humorist is a comedian who does not have to be funny because he is, by acclamation, very, very wise.

Keillor graduated from college in 1966 so he is about the right age to have been in Vietnam. He is not obviously handicapped or homosexual. He is a strapping man who has been married three times so he must have gone and fought. Many less strapping and more sensitive young men were compelled to do so Keillor must have gone as well. And apparently, he found his experiences so personally profound that he has never once spoken of his military service during all of his many years of celebrity.

Keillor does not live in Washington but he was there last Memorial Day. He was in town to "show (his) patriotism by looking at exhibits at the Smithsonian," and the parade of loud motorcycles got in his way when he tried to cross Constitution Avenue. So he had to

147

wait. And, it made him mad as hell to have to wait. And, he decided he was not going to take it anymore. So, he told the veterans and the friends and survivors and sons and admirers of veterans what he thought of them.

"A patriotic bike rally is sort of like a patriotic toilet-papering or patriotic graffiti," Keillor wrote the next day. "Somehow a person associates Memorial Day with long moments of silence when you summon up mental images of men huddled together on LSTs and pilots revving up B-24s and infantrymen crouched behind piles of rubble steeling themselves for the next push," he explained. "You don't quite see the connection between that and these fat men with ponytails on Harleys."

"If anyone cared about the war dead," Keillor continued, "they could go read David Halberstam's *The Coldest Winter: America and the Korean War* or Stephen Ambrose's *Citizen Soldiers: The U.S. Army From the Normandy Beaches to the Bulge to the Surrender of Germany, June 7, 1944, to May 7, 1945* or any of a hundred other books, and they would get a vision of what it was like to face death for your country, but the bikers riding in formation are more interested in being seen than in learning anything. They are grown men playing soldier, making a great hullaballoo without exposing themselves to danger, other than getting drunk and falling off a bike."

Nattering nabobs and nit pickers might notice that Keillor was so traumatized by Vietnam that he has completely forgotten that it ever happened or that he was ever there or how Rolling Thunder got started in the first place. All of the left-wing establishment in this country has been similarly traumatized by Vietnam for decades.

Which does not in any way alter the fact that Keillor is speaking for the American ruling class. Some stupid people on the margins of society might think he is a fatuous ass but Garrison Keillor is still America's most beloved humorist. He does not have to be funny. He makes the big bucks because he is wise. And, what he thinks matters to people who matter. Like the current President of the United States.

President Obama does know about Vietnam. He read about it in a book. He may or may not be as astounded or offended by veterans as Keillor is astounded and offended. He would never say if he was. He did go out of town this weekend, though.

What is clear as glass is that Obama thinks that Vietnam was so long ago that it does not matter anymore. Vietnam has nothing to teach post-modern America, post-manufacturing America, post-victory America, post-prosperous America, post-fair play America, post-jobs America.

Vietnam is so yesterday. "So yesterday. So yesterday," to quote the very wise, postmodern, Disney creation Hillary Duff. "Laugh it off. Let it go. So yesterday."

We have to quote Hillary Duff here not because she is offensive or unpleasant but because she is what America is today. We don't make cars, or steel or television sets anymore. We don't win wars. We make Hillary Duffs.

And, the President is not about to argue with the way things are. He sees that Rolling Thunder is so yesterday. And, most of the country probably agrees with him.

Vung Tau

So, I run into the impossible traffic jam that the California Highway Patrol has created on the 405.

Somebody or another has abandoned a Tercel in the south bound carpool lane. Probably they ran out of gas. Maybe they stole the car and then they ran out of gas. Maybe the thieves are walking to go get gas for their stolen car right now. This is Inglewood. This is the sort of thing that happens around here every day.

But the Chippies are determined that no one should approach this possible terrorist threat. So thousands of cars must stop. Our freedom depends on it. Unless there is a traffic jam the terrorists win. Everybody agrees except me.

All the good, patriotic citizens stop but I am still subversive enough and free enough to notice that the cops are just arriving at this impending catastrophe. Everything is not yet quite shut down. So there is not yet anybody to stop me from cutting all the way over to the far right, northbound lane and just riding around the police.

Maybe a cop yells, "Hey!" But, that is the end of it. Not even the California Highway Patrol would ever mistake me for a terrorist. At least, not that kind of a terrorist.   And after that the traffic really isn't so

150

bad. Partly because so much of what should be here is still stuck behind me and partly because it is Palm Sunday morning. The transition from the San Diego Freeway onto the Ventura is effortless. And I am in a great mood because I am riding to my favorite event of the year.

For me, for almost 20 years, this run has marked the official start of the "riding season" in Southern California. Not that it is ever not riding season here. But, sometimes it rains. Sometimes the ring of mountains that surrounds this city is covered with snow and the only way out is through all that. But, today it is bright as a new penny and the temperature is going to hit the mid-eighties.

I don't get any farther north than the bright, green hills of Calabasas before I just cannot hold it inside me anymore. I have to sing. And, I will be the first to admit it. I am funny when I sing. Well, maybe some people might say it is frightening when I sing but I prefer to think of the sound that comes out of me as funny.

Ventura Highway, in the sunshine! Where the days are longer, the nights are stronger than moonshine! Doo, doo, doo! Doo, doo, doo! Doo, doo, doo!

I know. It does not look funny when you see it in print. But that is only because you cannot actually hear me. Imagine Bob Dylan imitating Meatloaf imitating Michael Jackson trying to drown out 115 decibels of slightly used, slightly modified Dyna Super Glide. Imagine that and you can decide for yourself if it is funny or not.

Me? I crack myself up.

Doo, doo, doo! Doo, doo, doo! Doo, doo, doo!

151

The traffic is light but from time to time it stiffens up. I find myself behind some good citizen in a little blue coupe in the far left lane who only wants to go seventy. There is a cluster of cars over to my right and I don't particularly mind. We are all violating the speed limit and I am not in a hurry.

Suddenly a white van pulls up next to me and cuts me off. I have to brake hard to keep from getting clipped and frankly, speaking for myself, I think it sets a bad precedent to let anybody get away with this. I thumb my horn for maybe ten seconds while the white van bullies the blue coupe out of his way and then I set off in pursuit. The white van sees me, too, and runs.

I am not sure what I am going to do and even if I was I could not say it here but I am usually prepared to do something. The white van runs. I chase. We get up around 95 before the van is trapped by traffic. He has to slow and I pull up next to him. Sure, there is a possibility he might try to run me over but I have already thought of that. Maybe I know the freeways better than he does. Maybe I am playing chess while he is playing checkers. I want to look at him, anyway.

When I pull right up alongside he doesn't look at me. In fact he isn't even a "he." "He" is a Korean girl who looks to be about 12-years-old and I can tell she is already terrified of me. Somebody must have fed her a load of misleading biker stereotypes. And, I don't actually want to knock off her mirror or put anything through her windshield anymore. It is usually good enough for me if people are afraid to look me in the eye.

And, yet I want her to remember this close call she has had. I want her to think twice before she cuts off another biker so I glance over at her and I scream with all my might.

Ventura Highway, in the sunshine! Where the days are longer, the nights are stronger than moonshine!

That does it. Sure enough she fights her way over to the right, as far away from me as she can get and I see her taking the very next exit. It makes me happy when I win these little contests on the freeway. It makes me feel grander and more important than I am. It makes me laugh out loud. I swear, the best I ever get is in sixth gear.

A few minutes later I see the sign for Camarillo Springs Road. I am headed to the Vung Tau Spring Run, sponsored by the Vietnam Vets Motorcycle Club –proudly and patriotically "Knocking You Out Since 1984."

The name Vung Tau was intended to be broadly ironic when this run started in 1992. Now, it has become obscure. So, I would not be shocked to learn that half the participants see no more humor in the name Vung Tau than in my singing.

Once upon a time, Vung Tau was the Asian Riviera. The French, who taught the locals to drink wine and bake good bread called it Cap Saint Jacques.

And, then there were a couple of wars and in 1966 it became an in-country Rest and Recuperation (R&R) Center. Vung Tau was a sanctuary for everybody: Americans, Australians, the ROKs from the Republic of Korea, the southern Army of the Republic of Vietnam, the northern NVA and the Viet Cong.

"Peace man."

"Fuck 'em all but nine."

"Six pall bearers, two road guards and one guy calling cadence."

For many guys, a couple of days in Vung Tau was as good as it was ever going to get in Vietnam. There was no laundry service, no television, and no air-conditioning. But, you could sleep in Vung Tau. You could close your eyes and go to sleep and dream on actual sheets on a metal cot with a real pillow. There was food in Vung Tau. Not C-Rations or LRRP rations but food on a plate. You could get a beer or a drink of whiskey in Vung Tau. The place had showers and flush toilets. Showers! Flush toilets!

You could even get a woman in Vung Tau. Probably, she cost you five dollars. Maybe less. Eighty-five percent of them had some interesting disease—gonorrhea, syphilis, shankroid, the dreaded Black Syph—but nobody cared because she was a woman. She was always little and mostly young and mostly pretty and cheap and she, whoever she was, was probably the last woman you were ever going to hold anyway.

Oh you knuckleheads. Dumb, dumb knuckleheads. Marching down the Avenue. Six more weeks and you'll be dead.

Vietnam might have been the last gasp of Iwo Jima, the ghost of Guadalcanal. There were two classes in Vietnam. Some guys lived like animals and fought like animals until they became animals. Some guys were REMFs: Rear Echelon Mother Fuckers. "Those REMFs in Vung Tau. What do you think they're doing right now?"

"Shit."

"Mother..fuckers! Probably drinkin' beer!"

The war did not last forever: Except for sixty thousand or so Americans and a few million Vietnamese.

Eventually, the United States of America decided to adopt as its official policy the wise words of the illustrious writers of the Smothers' Brothers Comedy Hour. We declared a victory and pulled out. The last American combat troops left on March 29,

1973 and Vung Tau went back to being the Riviera. And, it stayed that way for a little while.

Most of the bars closed down. Most of the whores drifted away. Every weekend a few hundred thousand people would drive the forty-five miles north from Saigon to swim in the spectacular, blue South China Sea.

French restaurants returned to the torn cliffs above this sea. Everything was repainted. The Buddhist temples became improbable shades of yellow and blue. The Catholic churches were white. This was during the two years while there was peace.

You know the rest. Disco. The culture wars. The lessons of Vietnam and all that.

I pull up to a booth at the end of the road. I pay my money and get my meal ticket, my headlight sticker and my wrist band. It must be eighty already.

You know exactly what this run is like because, really, there is only ever the one run. The clubs arrive mostly in packs. There are multiple chapters of some clubs. Others send only four or five guys. One club sends one nomad. The independents and the civilians and the loners on the fringe like me dribble in.

There is probably one woman for every seven men. A surprising number of the women are dreams. I don't see one nightmare the whole time I'm there.

There is an American Flag flapping in the breeze. There has to be an American flag and another flag with the POW symbol just under that. There are always between fifteen and two dozen booths.

As always, the Soldiers For Jesus Motorcycle Club wants you to know that Jesus loves you. He does not care how you look or what you have done. "Jesus Loves Bikers Too." The Messengers of Recovery are there to give back "what we so freely took before."

I have been around, looked, seen, remembered long enough that I am seeing dozens of people both

155

again and for the first time. The bodybuilders with big arms are still bodybuilders with big arms but now they have grey hair. The happy, friendly 230 pound guy is now a happy, friendly 260 pound guy. The little guy who would fight anybody smiles more than he once did. Many of the wives and girlfriends seem to have become new and improved.

One booth sells a selection of flip flops. Another booth has a very nice assortment of Bowie knives. Everybody gets a nice roast beef sandwich, some potato salad and a big spoon of chili. The chili was better last year. Sometimes there is music. Sometimes an announcer talks and talks. Many things I do not actually need are raffled off.

"Hi. How you doin'? Good to see you. Peace. Welcome home."

I walk up to a guy and give him a hug. Then I give him some money and he gives me a tee-shirt.He tells me to, "Hold it up."

I don't particularly care what it says. I just want it to fit. "Better make it a double XL. They shrink."

The front of the shirt advises readers to "Support Your Local Red and Black Dago." The back announces, "Fuck With One Answer To All." Which I think nicely sums up the whole idea of a motorcycle club.

Wearing this is probably going to lead to either my hospitalization or a really interesting story some night in some bar down on the Rio Grande. Maybe both. Sometimes you have to actually go out and earn your stories.

The Red and Black, as everyone already knows, is no longer just the one motorcycle club. Motorcycle clubs thrive on war and recession. Now we have both. Which explains the kid standing next to me with the red and black side rocker that says Iraq.

"How you doin'?"

"I'm doing good."

The clubs roll themselves into balls that leak around the edges. Officers from one club pay their polite regards to the officers of other clubs. The Vagos are out in force.

"Thanks for coming."

"This is great."

"I want you to meet...."

Not everybody gets a handshake. Every so often a spontaneous hug fest erupts. The more beer the more hugs. There is only the one run.

During the two years while there was peace the North Vietnamese outflanked South Vietnam in Cambodia, Laos and in the demilitarized zone. There was nobody to stop them.

A law called the Case-Church Amendment prohibited the United States from giving South Vietnam any aid that could be used for combat purposes. So, the South Vietnamese ran low on bullets and grounded a fifth of their air force.

Morale plummeted. About 30 percent of the South Vietnamese Army became addicted to heroin. Their officers sold it to them.

Toward the end President Ford asked for $722 million for South Vietnam. Congress said no.

The end began in March 1975. The North Vietnamese overran the Central Highlands cities of Kontum, Pleiku and Ban Me Thuot and on March 25th the great panic broke. A quarter of a million refugees tried to run, drive and run to the coast: East on Highway 19 for Qui Nhon; east on Highway 21 for Nha Trang. People claimed there were only a quarter of a million of them anyway—farmers, shop keepers, deserters, whores, Buddhists, Catholics, grandfathers, mothers and children. Fifty thousand of them made it to the coast.

The North Vietnamese Army followed them every step of the way and killed as many of them as they could. General Sherman said war is hell but he was wrong. Hell is a parade of refugees 140 miles long under artillery fire.

Everyone who has ever seen an air burst knows that it is the fiery foot of a big, invisible elephant, an elephant a hundred feet high. Boom! The fiery foot stomps down and a cloud of smoke and dust erupts. When the dust clears you can see the big, invisible elephant's foot has flattened everything. Boom!

Whole herds of invisible elephants ran through the refugees day after day. No, don't see refugees. You see refugees in commercials on television all the time. The word refugee has ceased to mean anything.

See mothers wearing white and black, sadly trudging along, alone, their faces blank, their white blouses spattered with brains. See exhausted men stopping by the side of the road to sleep, no longer strong enough to be afraid, using bodies for pillows. That is what you should see when you see the word refugee.

Then it got worse. Then the whole country unwound like a ball of yarn. Half of the Army of the Republic of Vietnam, a million men, just disappeared.

The panic stricken and broken refugees streamed south on the coast road, Highway 25. Some of them made it onto ships that sailed into the coastal cities.

War is an excellent business. Enterprising merchantmen packed the refugees into cargo holds, 8,000 passengers a ship. Everyone had to pay, 8,000 fares per ship. Then the freighters headed for the southernmost port. And, you already know what that place was called.

The North Vietnamese moved 26 divisions into the south. Qui Nhon fell on March 31. Tuy Hoa and

Nha Trang fell the next day. All of this stampede of humanity headed to the one place that must be safe, the one place the Americans were sure to defend out of decency, out of sentiment, out of shame. Everybody went to Vung Tau.

No one will ever know how many –if only there was a better word, how many—refugees died on the roads. At least a quarter of those who went to sea died on the ships—of hunger and of thirst and of depravity.

The army deserters threw away their uniforms but not their guns. They took what they wanted.

When the ships got to Vung Tau the locals seized their last golden opportunity to get rich from the war. They sold the thirsty refugees water for two dollars a glass. Four hundred thousand refugees swarmed into Vung Tau every week.

Even after Saigon fell desperate refugees continued to pour into Vung Tau. It was the last way out. Refugees with money to pay or something to sell crowded onto junks and trawlers and pushed out to sea and prayed that the Seventh Fleet would save them, that somebody would finally save them.

Most of them were not saved. Most of them died at sea or returned to port and were sent to camps where they could be re-educated. That was Vung Tau.

And all of that is what is now bitterly funny about the funny name Vung Tau. Funny the way I am funny when I try to sing. Funny the way people think I am when I spit out the word "communist." I am such a scream. I am such a right-wing oaf.

I am still me after all this time. I am a little different but mostly I am still the same.

I drop my money. I pay my respects. I start my Spring and I leave before the hard body contest. It is not that I do not enjoy looking at women or that I do not think the women here are worth looking at. Partly it is that when I look at them none of them seem to be looking back at me.

Mostly it is because I think I should write something about this run, about what I see and how it feels to be here, and just considering what I might say seems to put me in a rotten mood. Maybe the problem is God is punishing me with this bad mood because it is Palm Sunday and I came here instead of going to church.

Nah. That cannot be. I was happy on the way up. Whatever it is, I have to get out of here.

Fortunately the answer to all my moods and ills is sitting just over there in that parking lot. Nothing brightens me up like a motorcycle ride.

I skip the freeway. I have all the time in the world. It is still early in the day. I cut through lettuce fields and the herb fields over to Port Hueneme and the coast. Even at the coast it still must be 75. There is a two hundred foot sand dune on one side of me. Sometimes the road isn't more than a hundred feet from the waves. Sometimes I can look down on the Pacific Ocean like God. I can see everything clear and bright.

And, I am still not out of my mood yet. I should be happy by now but I am not. It is the defective part of me, I know. It is the part of me that is not normal but I do not mind. I can live with me just fine. Just fine. You should wish you were me. And, when I get like this, I do not give a damn who you are or who you think you are, you should never dare to look me in the eye. The only cure is to ride.

The foam is white as cotton. The ocean is a rolling, perfect mosaic of turquoise. Those waves have been crashing against those same brown rocks for the last 10,000 years. Nothing ever changes. Not really.

And, today the Ventura coast looks just like the South China Sea. The way Vung Tau looked once upon a time. And, some days I like to look at it when I ride. But, today I look away.

Bruce Rossmeyer

Bruce Rossmeyer, the millionaire Harley-Davidson dealer who owned Destination Daytona, died July 30th on the ride to Sturgis.

Rossmeyer was on Route 28, a lonely, 76-mile stretch of road in western Wyoming when a pickup truck cut him off. According to a spokesman for the Wyoming Highway Patrol, Rossmeyer was traveling with five other motorcyclists when the pack overtook a slow moving truck pulling a double-axle camp trailer. "The pickup slowed and activated his left signal," the spokesman said. "Four of the motorcycles passed to the left. When Mr. Rossmeyer attempted to pass, the truck made its left turn and he hit the driver's side door. The sixth motorcycle swerved to the right and avoided collision."

Rossmeyer was an auto dealer who opened Daytona Harley-Davidson in January of 1994. He eventually turned that dealership into a 150-acre tourist attraction featuring restaurants, bars, a motel and a wedding chapel. He enjoyed the business so much he opened a string of dealerships including New Smyrna Harley-Davidson in 1997, Grand Junction Harley-Davidson in 1997, Ft. Lauderdale Harley-Davidson in 1998, Harley-Davidson of Pompano and Aspen Valley

Harley Davidson in 2002 and Sunrise Harley-Davidson and Southern Thunder Harley-Davidson in 2006.

Rossmeyer was a large and charitable man who enjoyed being large. He appeared in a self-deprecating commercial with an actor in a lizard suit for Geico Insurance. He had flames painted on the side of his private jet and he had the Harley Bar and Shield tattooed on his arm. "Publicity is what sells," he told The Miami *Herald* two years ago. "It's a way to promote me and sell more bikes."

Rossmeyer, lived in Ormond Beach, Florida. He is survived by his wife, Sandy, five children and nine grandchildren.

Bruce Rossmeyer died with his boots on. He was 66-years-old.

Requiescat In Pace

Swat Murdered Russell Doza

There was another Swat murder last month in Tulsa. Russell Doza, 49, was the victim of the new American style of policing: Which is not so much malicious as it is a crude mix of self dramatization and brazen incompetence.

Doza is survived by a memo from the Oklahoma City office of the FBI that alleges that the Rogues Motorcycle Club intends "to retaliate for the shooting of one of the club members by the Tulsa County Sheriff's Office." He left behind hardly anything to show for his life except a motorcycle and a couple hundred mourning friends. And, of course a pool of blood on a floor.

Right now the Tulsa Police Department is investigating that puddle of blood out of existence. The leaked FBI memo is part of that clean up. The conclusion of the investigation will probably be that Russell Doza got what he deserved.

So far the cops are right about at least one thing. Somebody should retaliate. The Department of Justice should retaliate. The ACLU should retaliate. Anybody who gives a damn about truth, justice or the American way should retaliate. Anybody who can still manage to say, "truth, justice and the American way" without smirking should retaliate.

The retaliation should be that the three Tulsa County Sheriff's Office (TCSO) Deputies who pulled their triggers and the Tulsa County Sheriff, Stanley Glanz, and Brad Henry, the Governor of Oklahoma, should all have their front doors kicked in and be arrested some dawn. The arrests should be as punitive, humiliating, brutal and unexpected as possible.

Then after the governor flips – and he will flip – a RICO indictment should be contrived so that another fifty-five or sixty cops can have their doors kicked in. Their wives and their children should be terrified to the maximum extent possible. Their personal assets should be seized. They should all be thrown into cages and made to beg their elderly parents for bail. The bails should be set at just slightly more than the parents can afford. All of these defendants should be assigned complacent public defenders and after rotting away in jail for four or six or eight or ten months they should all be offered plea deals. The ones who insist on protesting their innocence should get the stiffest sentences.

The retaliation should be like that. Then, maybe Russell Doza will rest in his grave.

Russell Doza was a biker archetype. He grew up in Girard, in southeastern Kansas. His childhood was comparatively disadvantaged. He became estranged from his family and according to news accounts in Kansas he "moved around between several northeastern Oklahoma towns." About twenty-five years ago he began moving around with other bikers. He met his long-time friend Ramona Gregory then, too.

"He was a gypsy kind of guy," Gregory told the Tulsa *World*. "He didn't have a place to call his own. He had his (Rogue Motorcycle Club) brothers. The club was his family."

165

Doza was light on the world. He did not leave behind many tracks. He was featured in a story in a local paper in 2001 about the Rogues bringing Christmas gifts and Christmas dinner to a severely injured Tulsa boy and his family. "Something we couldn't pass up," Doza told the paper. "The opportunity to help one needy child. That's what we're all about, anyway."

He was convicted of selling drugs while in possession of a firearm and he spent a year in prison before his conviction was overturned. And, he was disabled. He made his way with the help of his friends but he was slightly disabled.

Doza died in the course of a "high risk," "dynamic entry" service of a search warrant for methamphetamine and marijuana. The choice to serve this warrant in this way was self-evidently specious.

Service of the warrant was "high risk" because it was executed on the Rogues' clubhouse. The Rogues, themselves, were considered dangerous because years of "intelligence" and official reports published by both state and federal report writers had alleged that they were dangerous. It is common in the prosecution and harassment of motorcycle clubs for experienced investigators to conflate accusation, generalization, suspicion and probable cause. And, sometimes cops just manufacture the unverifiable observations that result in "reasonable articulable suspicion" and the entrapments that lead to probable cause.

Sometimes the game between cop and cop victim is entirely semantic. Cops know what judges want to hear. Defendants do not. Usually what judges want to hear are specific words and phrases that turn accusations into magic spells.

The affidavit that supported the search warrant on the Rogues club house was a magic spell that was intended to make this service "high risk." The supporting affidavit and the internal, officially secret, paper trail within the TCSO describes the club house as fortified; predicts firearms on the premises; predicts the presence of military weapons and ordinance on the premises; describes what is officially "sophisticated counter-surveillance," which is to say that there were security cameras; and suggests that the club house might be booby-trapped.

All of this ass-covering mumbo-jumbo was further supported by pretentiously documented surveillance including photographs and insider information from a "confidential informant." The warrant service was executed at "about seven-oh-six" in the morning, as a shaken police spokesman described it.

Technically this was a "knock and enter" warrant. Executing the warrant when everyone was asleep guaranteed that none of those inside the structure would have time to respond. And, that lack of response was half of the indispensible magic that allowed this Swat team to make a "dynamic entry." Dynamic entry is the police euphemism for what they do when they break in through your doors and windows, toss "flash-bang," smoke and gas grenades around like waffle balls and routinely kill your pets.

The magic words that allow for dynamic entry in the execution of a search warrant for drugs are "preservation of evidence." The legal theory is that unless police enter immediately Sweet Sweetback and his militant "soul brothers" are likely to flush their "stash of pot" down the toilet. The public relations reason, which is all you are likely to read or see on television, is that local police officers must use military "shock and awe" against American citizens so that the police can be protected from the people.

Police everywhere have embraced new media so it is not surprising to discover a Facebook page titled "I Support The TCSO Deputies." After Doza's murder, comments on the page enthusiastically endorsed his execution. "Warrant Service Ends With One (Bad Guy) Dead," a headline announced. "My prayers are with the deputies who put their life on the line, and I am glad they made it home to their families. My prayers are with you," one fan of the page wrote.

"Good job guys!! Glad the good guys didn't get hurt," a pretty woman added.

Another woman agreed, "Great job guys. Stay safe out there!"

There are 833 fans of the TCSO and it seems not to have occurred to any of them that Russell Doza's life was at least as valuable as the lives of the men who killed him. Most of them would probably be shocked by the notion that rootless, drifting, self-sufficient, anti-authoritarian, anti-materialistic, generous, honorable Russell Doza might be more important to the salvation of America's soul that any number of Tulsa County Sheriffs. "Great job," another fan wrote about Doza's death. "God bless TCSO."

Ironically, many police cars in many parts of America still wear a slogan on their sides which reads, "To Protect and Serve." And many very young and very old Americans still think the slogan refers to the duty of police to protect and serve the public rather than the other way around. And, that is only one of many ideas about the mission and responsibility of Swat that has been turned on its head since a cop named Pat McKinley invented the Los Angeles Police Department Special Weapons And Tactics (S.W.A.T.) Team forty-five years ago.

The original concept of Swat, during the quasi-revolutionary 1960s, was to provide Los Angeles with a viable response to snipers – like the handful of murderous psychopaths who popped up during that decade. Swat was also trained to rescue hostages and provide an efficient response to situations like the

Symbionese Liberation Army shootout. The Swat concept "evolved," McGinley later wrote, to become a way "to reduce risk to the police forces involved, to the suspects and to the community at large."

McKinley went on to become Chief of the Fullerton, California Police Department. In 2002, he was one of the authors of an evaluation of Swat deployments in California named after the State Attorney General at the time, a man named Bill Lockyer.

The *Lockyer Report*: "Was precipitated by a tragic death of a young male during a Swat operation. This death, though accidental, compelled law enforcement to engage in critical self-analysis with respect to the utilization of Swat teams. The Commission was deeply moved when this victim's family appeared at the Commission's public hearing. The Commission pledged to the family, to the Attorney General, and to the people of California that something constructive and lasting would come from their tragedy."

"Law enforcement operations are not military operations," the report states bluntly. "There is not an acceptable level of casualties, particularly of innocent bystanders." The point of Swat, its inventor believed, was to keep dangerous suspects from escaping while "trained hostage negotiators" used "verbal tactics." When a Swat team behaves professionally, the report argued, "Seldom are physical tactics necessary, and even then the actual firing of shots rarely occurs."

In the eight years since the *Lockyer Report* was published in California, other states have remained blind to the excesses of Swat.

There is no national consensus on what a Swat team even is let alone how and when one should be properly used. There is not even a consensus in Tulsa County which has both a city Swat team and a county Swat team. Nationally, Swat operational plans are often a ludicrous parody of the kind of cop speak Mike Judge satirized in *Idiocracy*. Their deployment is casual. And, their tactics and weapons are military tactics and weapons that are appropriate if the idea is to find, engage and kill an enemy but absolutely wrong if the idea is to minimize conflict and keep the peace.

In practice, Swat is how police departments bully and terrorize the American underclass, dissenters and other enemies of the police. Swat team members shamelessly describe themselves as "elite warriors" and seem to want to emulate Delta Force Operators. Delta is the often glamorized, Special Forces Detachment that carries out covert and clandestine operations on behalf of the Central Intelligence Agency and the United States Special Operations Command.

Swat operations also provide inherently dramatic footage, for content hungry television news broadcasts. Swat stories are easy stories. And, reporters who create these "news accounts" must either gulp and swallow real good or lose access to the only sources who will talk to them. The result has been a virtually unexamined escalation of Swat atrocities.

In November 2006, a 25-year-old Marine veteran and member of the Pagans Motorcycle Club named Derek Hale was executed by a Swat team in Wilmington, Delaware during the service of a search warrant for *indicia* of his membership in a motorcycle club. Last October, another Pagan named James Hicks was executed by members of a Swat team serving another *indicia* warrant in Virginia.

In July 2008, the home a man named Cheye Calvo in Berwyn Heights, Maryland was stormed by a Swat team because Calvo had thoughtlessly carried a package containing marijuana into his home. The package was handed to him by a policeman in disguise. But it was a drug bust so, of course, dynamic entry was allowed. It was a typically nasty raid.

But, Calvo happened to be the Mayor of Berwyn Heights. He was stubborn enough and politically connected enough to shame the State of Maryland into what is called "the Open Swat Law." All Maryland police departments must now disclose statistical information about their Swat raids. That disclosure has been reluctant but apparently complete and on February 24, the Baltimore *Sun* published a summary of information about Swat deployments collected during the final half of 2009. It is the first such disclosure in the country.

In six months, or 183 days, Maryland deployed Swat teams 804 times. "Police forced their way into 545 houses," the *Sun* reported, "seized property in 633 of the raids, made arrests 485 times and discharged their weapons five times. In the six months studied, seven civilians were hurt but none killed, and two animals were injured and two killed."

"Of the 806 raids conducted in the six-month period, more than 94 percent stemmed from search or arrest warrants." Only six percent responded to bank robberies, hostage takings, barricades and the other kinds of emergencies Pat McKinley had anticipated when he imagined Swat.

The way Russell Doza was disabled was that he was deaf. He almost died in an explosion. He survived but most of his hearing did not. He wore two hearing aids. He took them out when he slept.

So he slept through the dynamic entry. And when he died the only witnesses were police. Publically released accounts of the murder are remarkably consistent. None of the police participants have ever heard of the movie *Roshoman*. They have their stories straight.

Three Swat team members, Deputy Lance Ramsey, Corporal Tom Helm and Sergeant Shane Rhames found Doza asleep on the floor. They are all

171

experienced cops. Last year a local civic organization, the Sertoma Club – which "exists for the high and noble purpose of service to mankind" – named Ramsey "Deputy of the year."

The shaken police spokesman, Shannon Clark, said that as Doza woke up he reached for a gun on a nearby bookshelf. A slightly embellished account describes how Doza actually picked up the hand gun and pointed it at officers. Police have not yet speculated on why Doza decided to commit suicide then, there and like that. Most people do not have that reaction to even the worst dreams. When most people outside a combat zone awake they usually expect to live at least through breakfast.

Doza's old friend Ramona Gregory told the *World* that she thinks he was acting in self-defense. "Coming out of a dumb sleep, you're going to reach for something to protect yourself," Gregory speculated. "Automatically, if he has a gun to protect him, he's going to reach for it."

But, what happened might have been even simpler than that. It is plausible that as he was startled awake, Doza forgot about the gun on the shelf. As the deaf man opened his eyes he saw three fantastic figures dressed up like children on Halloween. They were shouting commands at him that he could not hear. So without thinking, without being given time to think, he reached for his hearing aids. So he would know what these officers were commanding him to do. So he could comply with those commands. And, then the police killed him.

The subsequent search found no drugs.

Who The Tulsa Sheriffs Killed

Russell Andrew "Roc" Doza was born in Munich, Germany on January 16th, 1961. He was named for his godfather, Russell Andrew Hall. His father was a career soldier and his father and his mother were often separated.

When Russell Doza was about two, he asked his mother, Leona, for a glass of Kool Aid. His mother, seeing the boy's brightness, possibly in hopes that he might someday become famous, insisted that Russell repeat an advertising slogan that went, "Kool Aid! Kool Aid tastes great! Wish I had some! Can't wait!" The baby refused. So his mother beat him. His four brothers and sisters watched. Russell Doza never said a word and eventually his mother stopped when her arm grew tired.

After his father divorced his mother, three of his siblings went with his father. So he lost half of his family. Russell and his brother Francis moved to Phillipsburg , Missouri with his mother. She refused to allow the boys contact with their father and she eventually married a man named Leonard Decker, who is remembered to have had a temper. He beat and abused both boys.

Like the lowly private, Russell Doza endured. He managed to graduate from high school in Girard, Kansas. Last month, a classmate said "I will always remember his great smile and wonderful laugh and the kindness he always showed to me."

After high school Russell Doza ran off to join the circus. After Russell's brother left home Leonard Decker beat Russell's mother into a coma with a baseball bat. No one seems to remember why. But she recovered and she also endured until she died on January 1st, 2005 in Lebanon, Missouri.

Little by little, Russell Doza made the most he could of the hand life dealt him. He lived with his brother until they fell out. He became an oil pipeline worker and a part time mechanic. He found and joined a family in the Rogues Motorcycle Club.

After he joined the Rogues, Doza lost about 90 percent of his hearing in an explosion. He wore hearing aids and he learned to read lips. He was arrested and spent a year in prison until his conviction was overturned. He had a dog who loved him. And, he was murdered by a Swat Team as he awakened on the morning of April 9th.

As of today, Friday, May 21st, 2010 the murder of Russell Doza is still officially unsolved. Oklahoma is one of the few remaining states without a Freedom of Information or Open Records law. An investigation into his death has been reported to be underway, but the records of that investigation are all secret. Both the Tulsa Police Department and the Tulsa Office of the Bureau of Alcohol, Tobacco, Firearms and Explosives have been rocked by corruption scandals in the last six months. And official statements about his murder are contradicted by accounts from knowledgeable sources. There appears, as yet, to be no federal or state grand jury investigating his death. If a grand jury has been convened, as of yesterday afternoon it had not yet begun to actually investigate.

When judged solely by the content of his character Doza was among the most kind, generous and honorable of men. He was sleeping in the Rogues clubhouse when he died because he had come there to work on the clubhouse roof. An evil man is one without a single woman to cry when he dies. At least a half dozen women cried when Roc Doza died.

Also among his mourners was an Oklahoma District Court Judge named Bruce David Gambill and Tulsa Police and ATF Agents harassed them all. Men, women and children who attended his funeral were stopped, questioned and photographed.

After his death, when asked to comment, his sister Charlotte replied: "Your question should be, how did Russell survive his life? As a member of the Rogues. The club gave him order in his life. The clubhouse was an inn...his stay was shamefully shortened...his soul will ride the wind."

Another of the women who cried at his funeral wanted people who never knew him to understand that, "Your lives would have been so much richer for knowing him. Losing him covers my world in black, burnt, bleeding filled with ashes. It is a wound nothing can heal."

Russell Andrew "Roc" Doza was 49-years-old. He never knew what hit him.

Requiescat In Pace

The Derringer In Doza's Hand

There were three people in the Rogues Motorcycle Club clubhouse in Tulsa when it was shock and awed at dawn on April 9.

One of them, Russell Doza, was shot between seven and nine times and killed. He was shot in the side and the back. Two of the shots entered his neck around the base of his skull. Now the United States Attorney in Tulsa is trying to put the two survivors, Scott Lee Sollars and Albert Dee Ahlfinger, in prison for ten years each. Sollars and Ahlfinger are charged with being felons "in possession" of firearms.

Neither man possessed a firearm as most of the English speaking world understands the verb "possessed." American prosecutors routinely torture English as former President Clinton tortured English when he wondered "what the meaning of is is." Sollars and Ahlfinger are being prosecuted because they belong to the Rogues and they were there when Doza was murdered. Sollars and Ahlfinger were in the clubhouse with Doza. And Doza was killed because he was holding a gun. So Sollars and Ahlfinger were in a house with guns.

Assistant United States Attorney Joseph Wilson told the Tulsa *World* that his office "routinely reviews potential federal gun prosecutions and that these cases were selected because of the overall circumstances." Cynics probably notice that these cases are being prosecuted before the results of any investigation into Doza's homicide are announced. One friend of the Rogues characterized the gun charges as a "joke." It is not a very subtle attempt to intimidate the Rogues into shutting up about that fatal raid.

However, after a very long silence the arrest complaints and supporting documents do shed a little more light on what happened on April 9.

The affidavits that support the arrest warrants were written, or at least signed, by a Federal Bureau of Investigation Special Agent named Amy M. Kuhn. And, as is usually the case with these sorts of things the statements they contain are written in prejudicial and self-important cop-speak, which is the noise cops make when they want to sound important, professional and authoritative – like an actor playing a doctor in an aspirin commercial.

"On April 9, 2010," Agent Kuhn begins her tale, "members of the FBI Safe Streets Violent Gang Task Force and Tulsa County Sheriff's Office (TCSO) Drug Task Force executed a search warrant at the Rogues Outlaw Motorcycle Gang Clubhouse, 1826 North Kingston Place, Tulsa, Oklahoma. Due to considerable safety concerns, members of the TCSO Special Operations Team were requested to knock, announce, enter and conduct a safety clearing of the location prior to the execution of the search warrant. While an entry and safety clear of the location were completed..." Sollars and Ahlfinger were "removed from the premises" and not placed "under arrest" but merely "temporarily detained for (their) own safety and for the safety of the officers involved."

Kuhn's sworn statement includes the usual *pro forma* admission that these sworn statements always contain, which is that that some of what she swears is a true is a lie of omission: "I have not included each and every fact known to me concerning this investigation."

For the last two months, the raid on the clubhouse was supposed to be a search for "marijuana and methamphetamine." There were actually two warrants issued on April 9. They are both state warrants.

One was issued by Judge Wilma Palmer 30 minutes before the raid. In addition to marijuana and methamphetamine it also authorized a search for: Instrumentalities, monies, records, financial records, proof of residency, drug notations and unexplained wealth from the sale of controlled dangerous substances, monies and or items consistent with the diversification of wealth, firearms, financial records and drug notation and residency papers. In general, this is language that is used to accomplish the seizure of all written, photographic, financial and computer records so police can copy them, add them to their accumulated "intelligence" and inspect them at their leisure to see what they can use.

The first warrant names a member of the Rogues who was not at the clubhouse and has not been arrested.

The second search warrant, issued after Doza's homicide and after the clubhouse had become a crime scene, sought all the items in the first search and: Human bodies, DNA, blood, impressions, trace evidence, firearms, ammunition, bullets including spent projectiles, cartridge cases, explosive devices (and) literature or documents associated with explosive devices or materials.

Two additional suspects, a man and a woman, are named in the second warrant and neither of them was in the Rogues clubhouse that morning either.

The only occupants of the clubhouse that morning were the two men charged this week, Ahlfinger and Sollars, and Russell Doza. Immediately after Doza's murder an FBI Agent named Charles L. Jones questioned both survivors about the location of any weapons in the clubhouse. Neither man was Mirandized and both men cooperated fully with police. Both of them had just heard gunshots from inside the house and were obviously eager to prevent bloodshed.

Sollars told Jones he believed guns "might be" in the residence. Ahlfinger told the FBI Agent that he knew there was a shotgun behind the bar and that because he was a felon he never went behind the bar where the shotgun was kept. Ahlfinger also said he thought there was a gun in a locked safe in the house and that he thought there were probably numerous pocket knives in the house but no explosives.

Both warrants authorized a search for firearms. Implicit in Kuhn's affidavit is the allegation that neither the FBI nor the TCSO knew who was in the house at the time of the raid because they had to ask. It is more likely – unless this is the worst FBI Field Office ever – that the police knew exactly who was in the house when the raid was conducted; that an informant knew the exact location of at least three of the firearms and may even have planted one of them in the clubhouse himself; and that the point of conducting the raid then was to contrive the charge with which Sollars and Ahlfinger have now been arraigned.

Both men were arrested on state felony gun possession charges the day of the raid. The arrest report states that guns were "accessible to all subjects in the house." The state charges were dismissed earlier this week when the same charges were filed federally.

The four weapons recovered from the club house were the Harrington and Richardson 12 gauge shotgun Ahlfinger told Jones he could find behind the bar; a TEC DC9 ghetto blaster; an "SKS 7.62 rifle" which describes a broad range of bolt action and semi-automatic weapons but probably is meant to describe an antique, five shot, bolt action rifle; and a "Cobra Firearms .22 caliber handgun" which describes a very narrow range of firearms.

Cobra makes two .22 caliber handguns. One fires .22 magnum rounds and the other fires .22 long rifle rounds. They are both derringers. The guns are specifically marketed to bikers as self-defense weapons. The Cobra web site describes them as follows:

"Derringers have more than 100 years of popularity and they continue to top the charts in sales today! From the Cowboy Action Shooter to the Harley Davidson rider, there's a Derringer to fit your personality. Even Grandma likes a little Derringer in her purse. Cobra Derringers are beautifully handcrafted with a wide range of calibers and barrel lengths."

Actually they are all between three and a half and about four inches long, cost about $150 and are not very good guns. A common complaint is a heavy trigger. Another common complaint is that the trigger just falls out of the frame. Bikers like to carry them and sometimes brandish them but they are very rarely fired.

It is beginning to look like this will be the gun that investigators will try to put in Russell Doza's hand when he was killed.

The derringer might very well be connectible to Doza. He had a legal right to own a gun. There may not be a record connecting him to the weapon and it might still have been his gun. He might have bought it in a private transaction. Or it might also have been a "throw down gun" carried by one of the police officers on the scene.

180

The official account of Doza's death has always been that three Swat officers found Doza asleep on a floor and he picked up "a handgun," intending to murder them. So they killed him in self defense. But that account has never rung true. One of the reasons for the long official silence is that is that the official account has been flawed with obvious inaccuracies from the time is was first recited to reporters. For example, Doza was not lying on a floor. He was in a bed in a bedroom.

Russell Doza's hearing was very impaired. He was not quite deaf but he wore hearing aids and he used closed captioning when he watched television. That explains how he was able to sleep through the Swat raid. If he had known that a commando team had invaded the clubhouse he would have undoubtedly acted exactly as Sollars and Ahlfinger acted. He would have cooperated. But he was awakened and as he started to roll over he was shot. The top secret forensic evidence is fairly clear about that even if it is too dangerous for the Tulsa *World* to report. He was sleeping on his stomach, as he always slept, and he never had time to roll all the way over.

So the gun that was "observed in plain sight" that Doza is supposed to have brandished at his killers was either a bolt action rifle, a TEC 9 or a derringer. And, no one who knew Doza has ever described him as the sort of a man who sleeps with a TEC 9. So the most likely weapon that police can put in Doza's hand is a tiny, inaccurate, shoddy, .22 caliber, single action, two shot pistol.

It will be interesting to read the cop-speak description of how threatened three cops in body armor felt when they saw that tiny gun – if there ever is a publically accessible official report. But the description of the great derringer danger will hardly be the most interesting passage. The interesting part will describe the five seconds before that.

Nobody knows exactly what happened in that bedroom that morning except the three shooters. But for almost two months there has been a consensus of informed speculation about what probably happened.

Apparently, this informed reconstruction of events goes, the three Swat officers rushed into Doza's room. Roc Doza was sleeping so soundly the Swat commandos walked right past him. Then they decided the room was clear and turned to go. They might have decided to poke around before they left or they might have just turned to go. They might have finally noticed Doza at that second or the next. They might have laughed at the sleeping man and poked him in the back with the muzzle of one of their guns. They might have pulled the covers down from around his head with one of their guns.

And, that was when Doza awoke. Or, maybe they never saw him until he awoke. It was a dimly lit room and as he rose to see what was going on he might have looked like a Haji who had been lying in ambush in the desert sands. He might have awakened with a start but whatever he did he scared at least one of the cops. One cop fired first then they all fired and Doza was dead.

And then somewhere either the derringer or the TEC 9 appeared. Finding, or planting, it does not matter, the gun would have given the shooters the out they needed. Finding a gun allows the cops to claim self defense.

It would probably be easier to put the derringer – rather than the TEC 9 – in Doza's hand because it is a kind of gun commonly carried in the biker world. But then, putting the derringer in Doza's hand raises the most haunting question of all. In the dimly lit room they saw the derringer but they did not see Doza. They saw the four inch gun. They did not see the six foot man.

They did not see Doza but they saw the derringer in his hand. And then, acting in great fear for their lives, they killed him.

Edge Trap Law Suit

The survivors of two experienced motorcyclists are suing the New Jersey Department of Transportation and the New Jersey State Police for failing to warn the bikers of the manmade road hazard that killed them.

Jude Bihari, 52 and Ronald Ross, 42, were killed by the same "edge trap" in separate accidents eight hours apart near Exit 57 on Interstate Highway 295 in Bordentown, New Jersey last Wednesday.

Bihari was a motorcycle commuter who lived in Bordentown and was on his way to work. He was just entering Highway 295 at 4 a.m. when he hit the edge trap, lost control of his 1997 Harley, went down and was struck by two other vehicles.

Ross was a master Harley-Davidson technician. He was ejected from his motorcycle when he hit the edge trap about noon. He later died of massive head and chest injuries.

Both men are remembered very fondly, Ross, for example, recently cut off his two-foot-long ponytail and donated it to a charitable group named Locks for Love which makes wigs for cancer patients.

An edge trap is the result of milling one lane in a multi-lane highway before that lane is resurfaced. The milled lane often feels like ice or oil to motorcyclists.

When a road is milled poorly the resulting grooves may vary greatly in size and direction. The process also creates a lane that is two or more inches lower than the adjacent, un-milled lane. This disparity in the height of adjoining lanes is commonly called an "edge trap." Both Bihari and Ross were trying to escape out of the milled lane when they died. Bihari was trying to do it in the dark.

"We wouldn't have to go through all this if someone put a 75-cent flare down on the ramp," Ross' brother Robert told the Trenton *Times*.

There are no federal standards to ensure motorcyclists safety in road construction zones. No one in the federal government, which actively concerns itself with what kind of special hat motorcyclists should wear when they ride and how loud their bikes should be allowed to be, has ever heard of an edge trap. There are no federal standards on road milling. There has never been a Congressional hearing on the subject of motorcycle safety in road construction zones.

The New Jersey Department of Transportation issued a statement that said, in part: "The first priority of NJ DOT is to promote safety on New Jersey's roadways. The department will explore additional steps, beyond the current state and national standards, to further promote safe travel through construction zones."

The next day Timothy Greeley, the official spokesman for the Department of Transportation, said, "Obviously…the dangers posed by this type of situation are heightened for two-wheeled vehicles."

The week before the deaths, a Washington lobbying group named Transportation for America released a report that said New Jersey had the worst roads in the country.

The dead men's survivors are contending that the bikers were not adequately warned of the road hazard they were about to encounter. New Jersey is expected to reply that they were.

Brother Speed Pack Crash

Twenty-six members and associates of the Brother Speed Motorcycle Club were involved in a chain-collision motorcycle accident on Interstate 5 north of Portland, Oregon about 2 pm Friday afternoon. The crash happened at milepost 282 south of Wilsonville, Oregon.

A tight pack of 28 bikes was riding in the middle of three north bound lanes at about 70 miles an hour when two sport utility vehicles driving side by side panic braked in front of the pack for an unknown reason. Traffic was light, the road was dry, the sky was blue and visibility was good. The road captain and the leader of the pack, the lead two bikes, counter-steered around the SUVs.

The other 26 motorcycles did not stand a chance. An eyewitness described what happened next as "a pile of motorcycles."

Brother Speed is a three piece patch club with ten chapters in Oregon, Idaho, Utah and Montana. Everyone in the pack was from Idaho. They had come to Oregon to celebrate the 40th anniversary of the founding of the club.

Ten bikers were injured seriously enough to require medical treatment.

Herbert Sinclair, 48, of Heyburn, Idaho, and David Bowyer, 44, of Coeur d'Alene were helicoptered to separate Portland area hospitals. Sinclair is in Oregon Health Sciences University Hospital and Bowyer is in Legacy Emanuel Hospital. Both men are listed in critical condition.

Juan Ramon Mata, 60, Christian J. Gankema, 40, and Gary Pawson, 38 were also hurt in the crash. They were transported from the scene by ambulance.

Police have not yet named the other injured motorcyclists or identified the drivers of the sport utility vehicles.

Clackamas County Sheriff's Deputy John Naccarato described the scene as "a melee." Five ambulances, ten fire engines and five police cruisers responded. The northbound lanes of the freeway were closed for four hours.

Invaders Case In A Nutshell

The mostly secret government case, or cases, against various members of the Invaders Motorcycle Club staggers on.

The Invaders legal situation is probably easier to comprehend when it is seen as a single case. The "case" results from three drug related indictments in two Federal District Courts.

Last May, a major newspaper speculated that the case is really about a double murder discovered in Saint Charles County, Missouri in November, 2007. But, since it is a Federal case against a motorcycle club there is also a strong possibility that the case may be about nothing, or hardly anything, at all.

On June 19, 2008 a Grand Jury in Hammond, Indiana returned an indictment against 19 members and associates of the Invaders. This case appears to have been principally investigated by unnamed Drug Enforcement Administration (DEA) Agents "in Chicago." The principal spokesman for the DEA in the Hammond Case has been a comparatively novice DEA Special Agent named Michael Burke. At the time of the arrests Burke had been on the job less than five months and was assigned to the Merrillville, Indiana Field Office.

Although he was a novice cop, Burke was an experienced prosecutor. He had worked for more than six years as a state prosecutor and more than three years as an Assistant United States Attorney in Anchorage before moving south. In multiple sworn affidavits, Burke testified that the Hammond indictments began with information learned from a wiretap on the phone of an Illinois marijuana dealer named Steven R. Campbell. Although, the first two indictments did not include the word "marijuana."

The first Indiana Indictment charged Campbell and Richard "Tricky" Kasper, Timothy "Beefy" Bartruff, Stacy L. "Weirdo" Judd, Kathleen "Kat" Conley, Bonnie S. Bol, Koni E. Burgess, Kelly J. Elston, Kenneth W. Harris, Thomas J. Kerbs, Christopher P. Krug, Tawnee L. McCluskey, Richard W. "Scooter Boy" Mote, Stacy C. Simpson, Daryl D. "Noodle" Taylor, Jeri L. Wright, Jason G. White, Jeremy Joseph and Amanda Cooper with numerous drug crimes.

The 67-page indictment elaborated virtually all the crimes that can be associated with methamphetamine: Making the drug, using the drug, possessing the precursor chemicals that are needed to manufacture the drug, selling the drugs that were not consumed and talking about it all on a telephone or by text message.

A lurid, 50-page, superseding indictment returned on July 17 explained how ten of the 19 accused would transport crank from Indiana to St. Louis and Denver where the drug was "sold for profit." The Invaders, who like to say they are "the biggest club of its size in the world," claim ten chapters in Indiana, Illinois, Missouri and Colorado.

It was a conspiracy, the government charged and, "The object of the conspiracy was to obtain methamphetamine, secure monetary profits and satisfy controlled substance addictions...."

The word "marijuana" finally showed up in a third indictment filed in a separate federal case in St. Louis on January 15, 2009.

That indictment Edward John "Special Ed" Boroughf, Robert Allen "Silver" Turner, Victor Dwayne Ashworth, William Arthur "Will" Bellmore, Gerald Wayne "Breaker" Dragich, Donald Steven "Donnie" Emory, Stephen Patrick "Sticky Steve" Morris, Michael Shawn "Hoosier" Ashworth, Daniel Charles "Doctor Pepper" Inman, Timothy James "Rap" Rappleano, Raymond Edward "Nipple Head" Bodway, Gary Wayne "Treeman" Null, Ronald A. Young, Shane L. Rohlfing and again, in a third indictment Timothy Jay "Beefy" Bartruff.

These defendants were accused of importing more than "fifty kilograms of a mixture or substance containing a detectable amount of marijuana."

The Invaders case, or the multiple Invaders cases, hardly seem to make much sense when taken out of context. About the only thing that is clear is that Timothy Jay "Beefy" Bartruff is the odd man out. Bartruff is the lone defendant remaining in the Indiana case. He is now scheduled for trial in Hammond in April 2010.

One curious detail about the Missouri case is that every single defendant there except Bartruff has made a sealed plea and sentencing agreement with the prosecutor. None of the pleas will be unsealed until next month. And, that suggests that Bartruff, a former National President of the Invaders, might have lost his game of musical chairs.

Published reports about both cases have described the Invaders as a "white supremacist gang" and "major methamphetamine supplier throughout the Midwest." Although, there are published reports of a great many "white supremacist gangs" and "major methamphetamine suppliers" so it is hard to see what makes the Invaders special. But, the Department of Justice obviously thinks the Invaders deserve a good public smearing.

There have also been published reports that federal agents have been trying to infiltrate the Invaders for at least a decade. Defendant number two in the January indictment, Robert Allen "Silver Turner, contested his indictment on the grounds of double jeopardy. According to Turner's motion:

"On June 6, 2006, Mr. Turner pleaded guilty to Count I, possession with the intent to distribute marijuana on August 26, 2005, and to Count III, knowing possession of a firearm in furtherance of the drug trafficking crime in Count I," in an earlier marijuana trafficking indictment.

Turner pled guilty to something on October 23 but what he said he did is still a secret. The "Plea Agreement, Guidelines, Recommendations and Stipulations" are all "Filed Under Seal as to Robert Allen Turner."

Last May the St. Louis *Post-Dispatch* which is often correct – as a broken clock is often correct – reported that the government suspects that members of the club killed two men named Randy Greenman and George Whitter. The two men were lasted seen in a bar in St. Louis County, Missouri in the early morning hours of September 1, 2007. Whitter phoned his wife and said he was riding home with his friend Greenman and that he would be home in a few minutes. He did not make it. Skeletal remains of the two men were discovered later that autumn.

The *Post-Dispatch* also reported that Invaders were suspected of the 2007 disappearance and presumed murder of another Invader named Alan

Henry Little. Little, the paper suggested, had been "cooperating with law enforcement."

Last Spring, defense attorneys said they believed the drug cases were only filed as a way to coerce Invaders into aiding the murder investigations. As of mid-December 2009, no murder charges have yet been filed.

Escape From El Lay

The beach used to be where the poor people lived. And, even though the new houses here have become more expensive than Beverly Hills the beach is where some of us poor people still do live.

It is possible to stagger out of the waves, cross the broad strand and face a trophy chopper displayed, like a modern sculpture, in the front window of a $3 million beach house. Then if you survive that surprise, if you keep walking, in a few minutes you might just see me, the worst mechanic in history, ineptly trying to tune the carburetor of the plain, black, ordinary motorcycle I ride almost every day.

Not every house at the beach has yet been flipped. So some people, without actually naming names, who would not normally be allowed to move here now yet remain. The old, pre-Blackberry, lazy life lingers here like patches of mange. I know they are going to pass a law against me eventually. It is only a matter of time. Some guy with a pencil neck and a hyphenated last name is going to take my shack by eminent domain. I can see it coming.

But until he does, I can still fish for my breakfast here, off a pier, without a license, just as long as I don't mind the mercury and the DDT. The bars are numerous and many of the old ones feature both bullet holes and ghosts. The sunsets are terrific. Half the girls look like movie stars. The other half aren't bad. Everybody stays in shape. The old cops are still mellow. Most of the kids know how to swim out of a rip current by the time they are five.

The bad thing about the beach is that it is surrounded by El Lay. Virtually everywhere you want to go is somewhere, back east, beyond the silence after the end of the thirty-seventh line of Daffy Duck's favorite sonnet.

You dream the drill in your sleep. Check the saddlebags, strap on the Tee-Bag, Windex your sunglasses, warm up the bike. Oops! Forgot to open the petcock. Put on the jacket and the plastic hat. Run a couple of signs. Stop and buy gas. Spill some. Curse. Wipe it up. Curse. Put your war face on. Start splitting lanes between the cars. Guard your space. Never back down. If they're afraid of you, they will not try to kill you.

A perfect, sapphire, 1958 Mercury coupe will not let me pass. This driver needs more than one lane. I have to look and when I do I don't say a thing.

The driver is a slim, dark-haired girl. Maybe she is nineteen. And, she cannot drive straight because she is slamming a giant, breakfast burrito down her throat while she drives. She has to be Chicana. This has to be her Papis's car. Only a Mexican man of a certain status and attitude owns a perfect, sapphire '58 Mercury. And, there is nothing I can say or do to her that will make her feel half as bad as she is going to feel when she has to tell her old man she had an accident in his beautiful car. So, I don't even try.

I pull up next to a black chick at a light. She has her wig sitting on the seat beside her and she is putting on her eyelashes. Personally, I have never gotten the whole thing with black women and wigs. She notices me looking down at her. Just a guess. Possibly she is one of those people who do not like the sound of motorcycle right next to their door. And, I soon learn we must be soul mates. My natural look is an angry glare. Hers too. Then, before we can make sparks, the light changes and I escape.

Every freeway in Los Angeles has a number and a personality.

For example, the 710 is the freeway of death. It runs north from the twin ports of Los Angeles and San Pedro to the warehouses east of downtown and the constant flow of big rigs wore out the pavement long ago. Most of the drivers are local short haulers and they are not very good at driving a truck. So, if you think you are a particularly good rider, or if you have been feeling kind of blue and you are not sure if you want to keep living or not, then the next time you are in El Lay you might want to give the 710 a try. Me, if I am going to Long Beach, usually I take the coast or the 110.

It is always the 710, the 5, the 10 or the 101, by the way. Other people in other cities may call these concrete traffic funnels by more formal names like Interstate 95, US Route 40 or the Massachusetts Turnpike; that sort of thing. But, your first month in Los Angeles you will learn that all the known world is but a spider web of lines. And, the lines without stoplights are named with a number that is always preceded by the indefinite article "the." And, each of the lines that has stoplights is called by an historic and unique name like Sepulveda, Imperial Highway, Foothill Boulevard, Santa Monica, Venice or PCH and none of them is every called "the."

The 405 is the most maddening of the roads that begin with "the." Thirty-five years ago Hunter Thompson claimed to have broken his steering wheel by pounding it in frustration on this piece of highway. Who knows what he would do now? The road has been improved a dozen times since then and each improvement has made it worse. Expansion seams stagger from lane to lane like bad handwriting. Stealth bumps and dips leave you punchy.

There is always a traffic jam in exactly the same place on the 405, at a place called the South Bay Curve. It is the broad bight of freeway between Los Angeles International Airport and the neighborhoods where the aircraft plants used to be; when there was still an aircraft industry in Los Angeles; when most of the world's planes came from the United States.

The first time I ever understood the idea of a modulated wave was at the South Bay Curve on the 405. The way it works is as soon as the car in front of you moves you must floor your accelerator. Everyone does this so no one from another lane can cut them off. Then after some distance, after a mile or a hundred yards, each accelerating car must panic brake.

For miles before and after the South Bay Curve traffic crawls like an inch worm. Cars rush and stop over and over. And, the closer they get to the South Bay Curve the shorter the waves of movement become. Ten miles south of here the traffic is slowing then lunging forward for a mile, then slowing and lunging forward again. Just ahead of me the traffic can only lunge ahead for a hundred yards before it must stop and wait.

I live here so I skip the South Bay Curve by leaning right onto the 105. Some people call this the Century Freeway, probably because it took a century to build.

The 105 is the newest complete freeway in the city and it is a delight to ride. It cuts through what used to be black Los Angeles, past the Hollywood Park racetrack, casino and the poker room where I sometimes fish; past the Fabulous Forum where the Lakers used to play; past the Watts Towers, through a five level, stack interchange where the 105 and the 110 collide.

You probably already know the 105, from appearances in such major motion pictures as *Hancock*, *Speed* and *Live Free or Die Hard*. You know, all of tomorrow's indispensible classics. This is the movie business' favorite freeway. For one thing the surface is still comparatively nice and clean so it looks almost pretty on a big screen. For another thing it is not near any movie studios so who cares when it is closed. Anybody who is anybody does not live here.

It only takes about 20 minutes to travel the entire length of the 105 because it has the highest speed limit of any freeway. Well, technically the cops think the speed limit is 65. But this is still a democracy and all the people who drive here agree the actual speed limit is just about 80. If you are going more than 80 you probably deserve to be stopped. But if you are only going 75 you probably deserve a pass because, after all, all you are doing is just trying to keep up.

And, then the fairy tale pleasantness of the 105 yields to the inevitable, grim, Stalinist reality of the 605.

The 605 is the gravel truck and trash truck freeway and so it is a special treat for those of us who consider windshields to be unmanly. The surface has been patched and relined until it is all bumps and seams. It usually moves faster the 405 but not nearly as fast as the 105 and the right three lanes are invariably full of lost truckers with broken speedometers. Some trucks like to go 30. Some trucks like to go 65. None of them have been washed since before the waning of the Clinton Administration.

Last week, the 605 was also the freeway with the most debris. It escapes from the trash trucks and most of it is comparatively benign. Only rarely does one encounter worn-out washing machines.

A plastic, grocery bag dances and drifts in front of me like a drunken bug. I counter steer left, then right, then just manage to catch this thing with the left, lower front of my motorcycle. I know from experience this could be worse. The bag could, at that very moment be welding itself to my hot pipes. Instead it has only wrapped itself around and around my shifter, my peg and my boot. This bag has found me and now that it has found me it loves me. It loves me so much that it never wants to let go and it coos to me like a torn flag in a hurricane.

Maybe I can shift if I have to. Maybe not. I don't have to find out yet. I am loose. The ride is loose. The bike is loose. I don't mind the bag. I love the ride. I love the wind. I do not even give a damn about the bits of gravel pelting me in the face.

But I probably should do something about that bag so I pull my three dollar, Pakistani, imitation Buck knife from its sheathe with my left hand and push the lock button on the back and flick it open effortlessly, gracefully, almost eloquently because I am loose. I am a great calm in the center of raging storm of traffic and gravel and trash.

I reach down and cut at the bag, hit a bump, relax, stay loose, steer the bike down a dip and through a curve and then when the road is almost straight and smooth I reach down again and cut some more. Then I wait, loose and calm, until I reach down again and cut some more and cut some more until the bag flies free.

"Bye, bye, baby!" And I laugh. Nobody knows I have just performed this little stunt but me but I still feel like I am up on a big jumbotron up in the sky anyway. I am so impressed with myself! I am a motorcycle god!

I get impressed with myself sometimes. It is an old, familiar banana peel. Maybe next I will pop a wheelie on the 605. Why not? Hell! I can do any damn thing on a motorcycle! Anything!

Anything except close this cheap, damn, imitation Buck knife. "Ouch! Damnit!" Without stabbing myself in my damned leg. "Goddamn Pakistani piece of crap!" Finally I have to take my right hand off the throttle to close the knife. I don't even try to slide it back into the sheath. I just shove it in my pocket. And, then I am impressed with myself some more because I have done this without running into a wall.

See, the way I figure it, the secret of my astounding brilliance on a motorcycle is that I am loose and the bike is loose. I just spent half a day working on it and my bike is running great.

It is running so great that I suddenly realize that I have been tooling along in fifth and I still have another gear. So I shift up and the bike is running even better than before. And, then I realize I wasn't even in fifth. Probably almost the whole time I have been on the 605 I have been running in fourth and I am now still only in fifth. So I shift up again and I just own that traffic like a torch owns butter.

I am loose and the bike is loose and I am almost through the worst part.

At its northern end the 605 becomes the 210 speedway. The 210 east of here is actually the newest piece of freeway in Southern California. It is mostly wide open, mostly smooth concrete with mostly bump free lanes wide enough to actually drive a truck through.

The 210 passes through or by the old ranching and farming towns east of what used to be the big city. Less than a lifetime ago, towns with funny names like Pomona, Fontana and Rancho Cucamonga provided half of America's oranges, most of the west's grapes and wine and half of California's beef and milk. Now all of that is gone to real estate development. Now the farms and ranches are just another 200,000 houses to flip or foreclose.

Debris builds up on the 210 but it is mostly in the left shoulder and the left shoulder is wide. The second trailer tire I see catches my eye. One is a phenomena. Two is a coincidence. I take the third to be a trend and after that I start to watch for the wreck of a trailer. I am riding to Laughlin, for the annual run, so maybe the wrecked trailer is carrying a half million dollars worth of custom motorcycles. Wouldn't that be interesting? I wait. I look but I never see.

All I see are rain grooves and burn scars from long ago wrecks and the bright pink tattoos of botched bank robberies and the traffic.

About sixty-five miles from the coast the 210 blends into the 15.

As you probably already know, the north and south roads of the interstate highway system all end in the number five. The lowest numbers are in the west. The highest in the east. The 5 runs from the Mexican border, through downtown Los Angeles and up to Vancouver. The 95 runs from Miami to New Brunswick. There are ten of these great north-south roads in all and two of them cut through Los Angeles. The next one, the 25, runs up from El Paso through Albuquerque and Denver. Then the 35 connects Kansas City and Minneapolis.

The 15 is the road to Vegas and Salt Lake and about the time you pass a cute, little, minor league ball park called the "Epicenter" in Rancho Cucamonga you start to notice that even in April the San Bernardino mountains are capped with snow. Most days the high altitude winds stumble off these mountains and cross the 15 approximately here. On a perfectly calm day you are likely to find a 20 mile an hour cross wind. On windy days the trucks struggle to stay in their lanes.

For as long as I dare I stay a little over to the right where it is easy to avoid the notice of the California Highway Patrol. But a mile or so before the weigh station at the foot of the Cajon Pass I get as far left as I can. If you are riding a Harley this is where you pass everybody.

The Cajon Pass used to be the far edge of Los Angeles. Now it is only the far edge of the Los Angeles Basin.

If you flew into the city a decade ago, about the time you were told to fasten your seat belt and stow your tray you could look out the window and see desert one minute and city the next. Below you for as far as you could see would be the infinite lines of a city. And, all of those lines are what I have just ridden through.

But now there is still more. Now El Lay boils over its natural boundaries.

I climb something more than 3000 feet in six or seven miles. The big crank and the big cylinders eat the altitude. I don't even downshift.

I am distracted once. I always stare at the ugly scar part way up the pass. I don't pray to it but when I look at it I feel a little afraid. It is so big and I am so small. It is the San Andreas Fault and it is exactly here that Los Angeles will fall into the sea. It is exactly here, sometime, three seconds from right now or three hundred years from right now, that the earth will suddenly jump ten or fifteen or thirty feet.

And, I do not want to be here then so I always look for it so I can open up the throttle and hurry past. Everybody hurries.

Then the first thing you see when you crest the pass at 4,100 feet is a kind of a yucca called a Joshua Tree.

The old Mormons called them "Joshua" because they thought the plants looked like the Old Testament prophet waving to them. "Hey, y'all! This way to the promised land!" Joshuas are the signature vegetable of the simplest and most brutal American desert. In the winter the temperature in the Mojave drops to twenty. In the summer, the temperature on a Harley on the black top can break one-fifty.

I have had four motorcycle accidents. I flipped a bike once. But, I think the closest I have ever come to actually dying on a motorcycle was probably crossing the Mojave without water, with a stuck throttle, in the middle of the day at the end of July. "It is dry, dry," a crazy poet named Sylvia wrote about this "mad, straight road." And, now El Lay is even here.

Technically this is San Bernardino, not Los Angeles, County and the city is a string of towns that culminate in a place called Victorville. Victorville is one of the old railroad towns that once dotted the Mojave. Most of them are gone now, or mostly gone.

There actually used to be more people in the Mojave; ranchers, homesteaders, Indians, prospectors and railroad men. This was one of the last spots in the west to become civilized. During the depression, while they were making Westerns down in Hollywood there were still high noon gunfights up here. Off there to my left there is a 131 mile long wagon road that people just forgot about for about 75 years.

Then Route 66 and the Great Depression changed everything. People left the high desert for jobs down in the city. And, only now are they coming back as the city grows.

I always stop in Victorville. I don't have to but I do. Habit. I am very habitual. The less I think the fewer chances I have to make a mistake.

I used to have a bike with a peanut tank and I got in the habit then. I always stop at the same station on Roy Rodgers Drive, near the Harley dealership. Right there, I am about 100 miles from the coast.

You can actually start to see the desert after you clear Victorville. Most of what I can see are creosote bushes. The occasional tall sticks shaking in the wind are called ocotillo. I don't know if they have an English name. This time of year the desert is fading from yellow to olive drab. The creosote, the poppies and the dandelions all flower yellow out here because that is the bees favorite color. Sometimes you can spot flashes of purple lupine.

Even here at the lip of the desert the city traffic continues. The thing to do in Victorville seems to be to drive on to Barstow as fast as possible and then race back again. Barstow is about 135 miles from the coast and when you get there you have a choice. You can either turn around and go back to Victorville which I guess is what most people do because that explains the traffic. Or, you can stay on the 15 and ride to Vegas or you can pick up the 40 at its western terminus and head out into the empty zone.

Of course, since there is a big bike event east of here and thousands of motorcycles will be heading this way, the State of California has chosen this week to close the transition road from the 15 to the 40. A traffic jam builds for miles. It does not oscillate like a wave. Everyone seems to creep.

I see a couple on two Sportsters wearing very large helmets and worried frowns. I pull up next to them and I shout, "Follow me!" I am not trying to be rude. I am only trying to be friendly.

I have passed this way many times and I know how to scoot through traffic and what to do when I get off freeway. It is a simple matter of a right and then a left and then another right and I am almost through Barstow on old Route 66. It is now a ruined, broken memory of a road but it gets me to the 40 in about five minutes.

When I pull up onto the on-ramp I glance over my shoulder and I discover that the couple on the Sportsters did not follow me. I get it. I am not that stupid.

Many days there is just something about me that many people do not like. Some days there is something about me that most people don't like.

But, now I am alone. And, I do not care. I head off across the desert alone. All I care is that I am finally out of El Lay. And, like Byron in the desert, for an hour or two, I might forget the human race."

Longrider Pauses In Yuma

Look, no matter how crazy you think you are there is always going to be some dude out there who is crazier than you. Ride a Harley long enough and you will inevitably come face to face with that.

Currently, the *numero uno*, stone cold *loco* longrider in all the land is a former Wisconsin politician named Dave Zien. Zien served in the state Assembly from 1989-93 and in the state Senate from 1993-2006. After he lost his last election Dave quit shaving. And, now he has come to resemble the trapper who, even the other trappers think, has maybe been up in them mountains by himself a little too long.

Zien is 58. He was a Sergeant in Vietnam. And, he says he has been riding since 1962, when he would have been 12, so he probably has you beat right there. By his own count, Zien had two million miles riding one motorcycle or another about a year ago. That's an average of 45,000 miles a year every year for 45 years. Do his ears ever ring do you think?

Zien has had similar adventures to what we all have had except because he rides so much he has had his adventures in bunches.

For example, he survived a collision with a deer. How many guys do you know who can say that? So, after the deer he started carrying a bible on his bike. For luck. As a kind of a prayer. Zien thinks it was that bible that saved him the second time he hit a deer.

And, who can argue with him? Maybe the first time Dave lived because Dave was lucky and Dave was good but that second time it had to be the Lord.

In 2003 Zien put 31,000 miles on his motorcycle in 31 days. Appreciate that for a few seconds. Thirty-one thousand miles in 31 days.

For many riders 31,000 miles involves at least a dozen motor oil changes, a half dozen primary and transmission fluid changes, new brake fluid three or four times, at least two new tires and at least 20 hours of tightening up everything that is about to fall off, lubing the cables, changing the plugs and staring at the beast and wondering how it is going to try to kill you this time.

Then there is the actual riding, which has to average at least 14 hours a day. It depends where you ride. Some places are harder than others. If you are trying to put a thousand miles a day on a bike in Los Angeles you can't do it in this Los Angeles. You have to go for it in the Los Angeles that is on the planet that has 48-hour days. Probably you couldn't ride a thousand miles a day every day for a month but Zien did –on a 1991 FXRT Sport Glide. So it was perfectly natural, at the beginning of August, for Dave Zien to look down at his odometer and see that it read 969,000 and then to wonder what we all wonder. "I wonder, how high does this thing have to go before it gets back to zero?"

Zien managed to add another 19,000 miles to his score before he blew out his engine on October 16, on Interstate 8 in Arizona, among the Saguaros and the abandoned jojoba plantations between Sentinel and Tacna.

"I remember it really well. Mile marker 48," Zien told the Yuma *Sun*. "I started getting heatstroke out there and black smoke was coming out both my pipes, oil dripping, it was horrendous, just a cloud of smoke."

It is okay, Dave. We've all been there. Some of us have even been there right there.

Soon enough, a kindly couple in an RV stopped to keep Dave company. He called Harley's Road America towing service and by a miracle, maybe because of that Bible he carries on his bike, he managed to get the operator who speaks English. So eventually, he got a tow into Bobby's Territorial Harley in Yuma.

Zien is still waiting on his new engine. He was supposed to be on Jay Leno's Tonight Show last night. Leno is a motorcycling enthusiast who had heard about Zien.

And, Zien had hoped to have the million miles on his bike by now so he could have talked about that on TV. But, he missed his chance. The Love Ride is also in Los Angeles this weekend and Zien could have gone to that.

The riding is probably better in Los Angeles this weekend than it will be in Wisconsin. Here, it is about 90. There is a light Santa Ana blowing. The sky is almost blue. Zien is missing this weather, too. It seems like a shame.

Probably by now Zien's his butt is starting to feel real strange. Probably, by now he is starting to pace around a lot, snap at people and get edgy.

After 46-years it may have been the one thing Dave Zien had yet to learn about riding a motorcycle. Sometimes even the craziest longrider of us all cannot ride everyday.

Why James Hicks Died

The search warrant that got Pagans Motorcycle Club patch holder James Marcus "Jimbo" Hicks, Jr. who was killed last week is still an official state secret. So is the affidavit which asked a judge to authorize the search.

So is the name of the Bureau of Alcohol, Tobacco, Firearms and Explosives (ATF) agent who wrote that affidavit. It is not yet an official secret that the name of the Resident Agent in Charge of the ATF's Richmond office is Brian Swann.

The details of this shooting are secret not because revealing them might jeopardize an ongoing criminal investigation but rather because they might jeopardize the bureaucrats responsible for James Hicks homicide. If they were made known there is a very slight chance that some policemen might be embarrassed. There is an even a remote possibility that one of them might lose his job.

Hicks' widow Cathy was standing right next to him when a cop pretending to be a commando shot her husband twice. It was the darkest hour before the dawn. The middle-aged husband and his middle-aged wife went to confront whoever was trying to break into their home. They went together. He picked up a varmint gun. She was standing so close to him she could "feel the wind" of the bullets that killed him.

Then the police kicked Cathy Hicks out of her house. They did not have the decency to let her hold her husband while he died. Hours later she had to go to a gas station to use a bathroom. Witnesses at the gas station said she was still crying.

The top secret search warrant, which nobody is ever supposed to see lists the "Items to be seized" to be seized from James and Cathy Hicks' home as "PMC members' colors and club memorabilia such as patches, shirts, cuts, jewelry, belts, wristbands, wallets, walking sticks, posters, glassware, statues, plaques, business cards or club cards and the PMC constitution or any document containing PMC membership information or PMC rules."

The warrant that precipitated James Hicks' homicide was a "Knock and Announce" search and seizure warrant.

In the United States, a warrant must be obtained before a search can be conducted in any place in which a person may have "a reasonable expectation of privacy:" Such as their home after dark. A warrant authorizes officers of the court to search for specific items at a specific place at a specific time. Search warrants are issued to find and seize contraband or evidence of criminal activity.

Only the judge who signed the warrant can explain why this warrant specified the intrusion of someone's home before dawn or what criminal activity Pagans "memorabilia" might evidence. According to Virginia law, under the conditions of this warrant the police were required to knock, identify themselves and then wait a reasonable time for the Hicks to open the door.

A Virginia State Police spokesman named Sergeant Thomas Molnar said last week that police scrupulously followed the law regarding these conditions. Molnar claims Hicks "confronted" officers with a shotgun, that he was "ordered" to drop the gun, that he "refused" to do so and then he was shot by an officer wearing body armor and a Kevlar helmet who was acting in self defense. Molnar was not there. Cathy Hicks, who was, said her husband never had time to lay down his gun before he was executed.

Last night, Richmond, Virginia television station *WTVR* announced it had lawfully obtained the "search warrant return and inventory list" from the Hicks home invasion. The items seized from the home included Hick's "shotgun, a bank statement, assorted photos, (2) motorcycle helmets, MC Club patches, 2 Pagan walking sticks, camera, Samsung video camera" and "assorted ammunition."

So that is why James Hicks was killed. That is why Cathy Hicks was shut out of her home for hours and compelled to grieve in a gas station rest room. For, "assorted photos."

Don't tell anybody. The warrant and the inventory list are secret.

James Hicks was buried last Saturday.

Dulaney Out Of Pagans Case

William L. Dulaney, a college professor who studies motorcycle outlaws, has withdrawn as an expert witness in the Pagans Motorcycle Club RICO case in Charleston, West Virginia.

Dulaney is a former member of the American Outlaws Association who has become a common source for journalists seeking insight into the outlaw world. He has appeared on *The National Geographic Channel*, *The History Channel* and *The Biography Channel* in the last two years. He contributed as essay to *The Mammoth Book of Bikers* and wrote a well known "history of outlaw motorcycle clubs" for *The International Journal of Motorcycle Studies*. A year ago the *Christian Science Monitor* quoted Dulaney in an article about the demise the Myrtle Beach Rally. Last October, the *Associated Press* turned to Dulaney for some instant insight into the Pagans case.

Dulaney, as opposed to most biker experts, clearly gets it. Last February, he stated that he was prepared to testify that:

"The Pagans Motorcycle Club (PMC) is not a criminal organization or a national
criminal organization. Instead, the PMC is best described as a series of motorcycle organizations

predominately scattered across the Eastern United States whose members are overwhelmingly not criminals. The PMC is a relatively small motorcycle club with chapters coming into and out of existence over time in locations limited to Florida, West Virginia, Eastern Pennsylvania, Ohio, Maryland, Delaware, New York, and Kentucky."

Dulaney's testimony would have provided a refreshing contrast to the ceaseless demonization of motorcycle clubs by cynical, and occasionally deranged, ATF and FBI Agents and other professional experts – like rap aficionado Chuck Schoville, President of the International Outlaw Motorcycle Gang Investigators Association.

Dulaney decided to withdraw from the case after what is called a "Daubert hearing" on May 10. While police are automatically assumed to be "expert witnesses" who can speak authoritatively about bikers, other witnesses who disagree with the police must prove their authority to do so. There are a couple of different standards used in the Federal courts to determine whether a witness knows what he is talking about or not. They are called "Daubert" and "Frye" Failure to meet the Frye standard, for example, is the reason why polygraph examinations are not admissible in federal court. The Daubert standard is designed to ensure that what the "expert" knows is, "relevant to the task at hand" and is based "on a reliable foundation."

Before an expert can testify he must submit to a trial within a trial called a *voir dire*. In this case it was a fight between Dulaney and prosecutor Steven I. Loew over Dulaney's credibility.

Loew wanted Dulaney "to produce the names of members of the Pagans
Motorcycle Club and other motorcycle clubs whom he had interviewed in preparation for

testimony in this case." Dulaney refused. The judge in the case, Thomas E. Johnston, agreed with Lowe.

The next day the defendant who had hired Dulaney, Richard Timothy Weaver, sent the court a formal notification that, "Dulaney asserts that he has a professional ethical obligation not to disclose those names. To avoid being required to produce those names, Dr. Dulaney has requested that he be withdrawn as an expert witness in this case."

Suppressing Indicia Warrants

The Department of Justice obviously knocked over a hornet's nest when it decided to indict 55 members and associates of the Pagans Motorcycle Club in Charleston, West Virginia. Maybe Charleston should be famous for its defense lawyers.

Last Thursday an attorney named Tim Carrico acting on behalf of a client named Eric W. Wolfe attacked the legality of *indicia* search warrants. Carrico called an *indicia* warrant executed on his client's home an illegal violation of Wolfe's rights "as protected by the Fourth Amendment and First Amendment to the United States Constitution."

Indicia (in-DISH-hee-uh) search warrants are issued to search for "signs" or "indications" that somebody the police already do not like belongs to a motorcycle club. The judges who issue these warrants assume that proof of membership in a motorcycle club equals proof of criminality. On the west coast, all the cool cops make an even more astounding logical leap. *Indicia* warrants in California, Arizona and Nevada often include boiler plate language that a warrant to search for items like "Support Your Local 81" tee shirts is a warrant to seek proof of "participation in a criminal street gang."

Thousands of *indicia* searches have been carried out in the United States in the last two years and the spectrum of results begins with burlesque and terminates in tragedy. The auto burglaries supervised by ATF Special Agent John Ciccone in a sweltering parking lot in Lancaster, California –in the Mojave– last summer as part of a frantic search for "MFFM" patches was almost funny enough to be forgiven. If Ciccone were French he would have already joined Jerry Lewis as an Officer of the Order of Arts and Letters.

The search of a paraplegic's home in Los Angeles around the same time by commandos in body armor and Fritz helmets and the subsequent seizure of his Mongols calendar was disquieting. The videos of the *indicia* searches that accompanied "Operation Quiet Riot" in Arizona and Nevada late last year were Altmanesque. All they seem to prove is that Hells Angels are very good natured when the police wake them up in the middle of the night.

The *indicia* warrant served on James Hicks' home last fall was tragic and contemptible. In the darkest hour before dawn, Hicks was awakened by the sound of someone breaking into his home. He picked up a shotgun and he and his wife went to investigate. When he was confronted by police in his kitchen he acquiesced to their demands that he put down his gun. When Hicks turned to lay his weapon on his kitchen table a "Tactical Team" officer shot him multiple times in the back and side and killed him.

His wife was dragged out of her home and away from her husband's body to facilitate the following *indicia* search. The search lasted hours while the widow Hicks grieved in the bathroom of a nearby gas station. The items actually seized included a "shotgun, a bank statement, assorted photos, (2) motorcycle helmets, MC Club patches, 2 Pagan walking sticks, camera, Samsung video camera" and "assorted ammunition."

Eric Wolfe's home in St. Albans, West Virginia was the target of a similar *indicia* search related to the

216

same case. Briefly stated, Wolfe's home was searched because he belonged to the Pagans. So proof of his membership was sought –in order to observe anything that might happen to be in plain sight after all his dresser drawers were pulled out and upended.

A supporting affidavit asserted that a man paid by the Bureau of Alcohol, Tobacco, Firearms and Explosives to spy on the club in Charleston had been beaten up by members of the club in New Jersey. And, that this beating "was a criminal act on behalf of or in furtherance of the Pagans." And, Wolfe was a member of the Pagans.

So, *voila*! A warrant was issued seeking "evidence constituting *indicia* of the Defendant's association with the Pagans Motorcycle Club;" specifically the seizure of club "colors and club memorabilia such as patches, shirts, cuts, jewelry, belts, wristbands, wallets, walking sticks, posters, glassware, statues, plaques, business cards or club cards, and the PMC constitution or any document containing PMC membership information or PMC rules."

Document searches are always interesting because they usually allow the search of personal computers. And every single byte on a personal computer is considered to be "in plain sight."

The motion Wolfe's lawyer filed last week notices that, "There is no allegation in the affidavit that the alleged subject racketeering enterprise is wholly illegitimate, or that such a large portion of its activities are illegitimate so that it could be considered, in effect, wholly illegitimate. Therefore, evidence of mere association would not necessarily aid in obtaining a conviction.

"The affidavit in support of the search warrant authorizing seizure of *indicia* of membership or association does not provide probable cause to believe

217

that the defendant has conducted affairs of the PMC, at least in part, through a pattern of racketeering activity.

"Consequently," the motion argues, "the search performed by the government of the defendant's residence and vehicle on October 6, 2009, for *indicia* of membership or association evidence was illegal and in violation of the defendant's rights" and that "all evidence located, seen, and obtained as a result of the illegal search must be suppressed."

And, these searches are unconstitutional.

The First Amendment to the Constitution guarantees a person's right to belong to any church or motorcycle club he wants. It also guarantees your right to read these words. It states: "Congress shall make no law respecting an establishment of religion, or prohibiting the free exercise thereof; or abridging the freedom of speech, or of the press; or the right of the people peaceably to assemble, and to petition the government for a redress of grievances."

The Fourth Amendment states: "The right of the people to be secure in their persons, houses, papers, and effects, against unreasonable searches and seizures, shall not be violated, and no Warrants shall issue, but upon probable cause, supported by Oath or affirmation, and particularly describing the place to be searched, and the persons or things to be seized."

Shameless Iron Pig

Ronald Smith, the well known Seattle pawn shop unit detective, police union official and proud patch holder in the Iron Pigs Motorcycle Club, is suing the Seattle Police Department for $169,800.

Smith alleges his department slandered him days after he gunned down and severely wounded an unarmed member of the Hells Angels Motorcycle Club in the Loud American Roadhouse in Sturgis on August 9th, 2008. Smith alleges he suffered emotional distress when Seattle Police Chief Gil Kerlikowske said Smith had used a Police Department Glock automatic pistol to shoot Joseph McGuire in the stomach and the leg. Smith maintains that he actually used his personal Glock automatic pistol, purchased from the Seattle Police Athletic Association, when he tried to kill McGuire.

Smith demands $150,000 to heal his emotional wounds. He also demands $19,800 to pay his lawyer and to compensate him for lost wages.

According to the suit, Smith only tried to kill McGuire because he was "defending himself from a violent premeditated attack, and he responded in a manner which was neither excessive nor unreasonable." Smith also believes his reputation was harmed when

219

then-Chief Kerlikowske called him an "embarrassment." Kerlikowske is now Director of National Drug Policy in the Obama Administration.

The Iron Pigs Motorcycle Club is a three-piece-patch motorcycle club comprised of sworn piece officers, prison guards, security guards and fire fighters. The club was founded in Oroville, California in December 2000 by disgruntled members of another cop club, the Wild Pigs Motorcycle Club.

The club intends to either parody or outdo other three-piece clubs. Members wear state bottom rockers and a diamond patch enclosing "99%." The club motto is "Never Let The Bastards Wear Your Down." Before the shooting in Sturgis, the club website proclaimed, "In our professions we are forced to deal with a lot of crap on the job; we don't need it when we play."

A Massachusetts criminologist and retired cop named Mitch Librett wrote one of the few scholarly articles about the strange phenomena of cop motorcycle clubs. The monograph, "Wild Pigs and Outlaws: The Kindred Worlds of Policing and Outlaw Bikers," was published in *Crime, Media, Culture: An International Journal.*

Librett sees "striking similarities in self-presentation" between cop clubs and other three piece patch clubs. "The colors, slogans, and monikers adopted by the members are often indistinguishable," Librett has said, "I really have to question why any police officer would feel that emulating the (outlaw) lifestyle is an attractive way to spend their free time."

About two years before the Sturgis shooting, Iron Pigs National Vice President Anthony "Kornbread" Barber explained the attraction to *WBOY* in West Virginia, "Some of us get a kick out of pulling up at a red light and watching people lock their doors."

220

The pugnacious Iron Pigs once sued a minor league baseball team in Pennsylvania, an affiliate of the Phillies called The Iron Pigs – after a common raw ingredient used in nearby steel mills – with trademark infringement.

Official and published accounts of the shooting differ radically from what eyewitnesses have described to this page.

Officially, Smith and four other Iron Pigs who were involved in the incident described themselves as being surrounded and attacked by Hells Angels. News media have described the attack as unprovoked. Charges were brought and dismissed against all five Iron Pigs. After months in the hospital, McGuire was charged with aggravated assault. He eventually pled no contest to simple assault in February 2009.

Uncontrovertibly, Smith has a long history of trying to bully Hells Angels. In 2005, Smith stalked, threatened and then charged a Seattle motorcycle shop owner named James Magnesi with threatening him. A tape recording proved that what had happened was that Smith had actually called him a "dirtbag," told him to watch his back and told him that belonging to the Hells Angels is a crime.

Witnesses have said that McGuire and one Hells Angels prospect were surrounded and harassed by the five Iron Pigs. Smith insulted McGuire. When McGuire punched Smith in the face and knocked him down Smith shot the Hells Angel twice.

Smith claimed to be acting in self defense because he reasonably felt himself to be in mortal danger. But none of the four other Iron Pigs who witnessed the fight made any effort to break it up or to defend Smith.

Waiting For SAMCRO Again

I am riding up through the high desert into the Eastern Sierras a week or so ago. The ride is always plagued with bugs. And, I have never owned a motorcycle with a windshield or a fairing or any of that crap so I am very aware of the bugs. At ninety miles an hour they explode like kinetic weapons all over my sunglasses, inside my nose, inside my mustache, on my teeth, on my hands, on my leathers and clothes.

I ignore them mostly. Because I am riding the bike. The bike doesn't ride itself. And, every so often I make a silly, high-pitched noise. But, I can't tell you whether I am cursing or praying when my face meets the bugs that might actually be small, hard birds.

When I came home and stripped off my clothes I found a horsefly under my scrotum. It seems that one, determined bug had somehow survived the collision with my cowboy boot, crawled up the leg of my jeans, struggled into my underwear, curled up under my balls and died. My old lady laughed. And, then she went on to imagine out loud all the species of insects it could have been. I took a shower and after I got out I more or less forgot about that fly.

I only remember it now because I am writing yet again about *Sons of Anarchy*, the brilliant, gritty, critically acclaimed, astounding work of sheer-fucking-genius currently running fifteen or twenty times a week on the *FX Cable Network*. The show's creator and principal propagandist is the prosperous actor and scrivener Kurt Sutter.

And, I have made the artistic choice of beginning this essay with a dull anecdote about a bug by way of explaining to you that, as a general rule, anything Kurt Sutter might say is to me as the buzzing of a fly. Not even a fly that would lose its life on account of me but just another fly. So I would not have noticed the 950 words Sutter published on his blog (SutterInk.com) last Monday if someone had not pointed it out to me. But someone did. And, then I read it. So here we are. Again.

I am really sorry about this. But I have found that it is never the things I say that make me crazy. Or, crazier. It is also what I don't say. And, most people who know me agree, I am already crazy enough.

Sutter more or less argues that if I don't like his television show I must either not get it because I am stupid or, worse, there must be something inferior about me – I must not be as far out there on the outlaw frontier as he.

Sutter spent last Sunday hanging out with Sonny Barger and the Cave Creek Crew. Barger's wife lent him a bike. (That has never happened to me.) Sutter and Barger signed autographs side by side. (I don't give autographs. It is easy. Nobody asks.) Afterward, Sonny and Kurt and some of the guys went over to Sonny's house. (I don't even know Barger's address.) I don't know if they had some beers or smoked some dope or did some lines or ate some hot dogs or sang some karaoke or what. Sutter only says, "I hung out and listened to these guys swap stories and critique the show."

"I gotta say," Sutter continues modestly, "the coolest thing to me was how much all these people love the show. I mean they really fucking love it. Every character nuance, every detail is not wasted. They are smart, sophisticated viewers who completely plug in. And they totally get and accept that it's television and that we take deep dramatic license. My favorite quote of the trip," Sutter continues, "came from one of the Cave Creek members, who blurted out this excited revelation, 'Sons is fucking soap opera...but it's our fucking soap opera.'"

I believe that what Sutter is implying here is that I am disconnected from my peers and estranged from my intended audience. Not that Sutter would ever actually say this to me. Sutter of course, has never actually heard of me. Somebody with a name like "Really Scary Outlaw" with a return email address like "writers at SOA dot com" is more likely to say this to me. Maybe "Really Scary Outlaw" knows Kurt.

In any event, whether he has heard of me or not, I have still heard of him. Which from Sutter's perspective might be worse. Because, almost out of reflex, after I read what Kurt wrote, I decided to watch his show again and write another review. You know? Like what you do when a bug lands on your arm.

The episode I watched was called "Smite" and I don't have the faintest idea why it was called that. Also, I took notes but they make absolutely no sense:

"Real estate developer. This looks like Azusa. 'Your body isn't producing enough estrogen. I'll write you a prescription.' Estrogen? Do the Grim Reapers mind that Kurt Sutter stole their patch? Suits, big cigar, more real estate chat, endless parking of motorcycles. Don't these guys ever take off their cuts? Ron Perlman wants some guy in a cigar store to pay him a grand a month.

"Perlman walks like he shit his pants and he looks like he can smell it. Don't any of these bikes have petcocks? Henry Rollins is some kind of thug. Some high school. Why is there a high school? No, it is supposed to be a jail. Kurt Sutter is mopping a floor. His name is Otto. Geez, Kurt! Throw straight punches! Straight punches! Oh geez! Kurt gets eye fucked with a broken mop handle. That is kind of interesting. I can see myself doing that to Kurt."

See what I mean? My notes make no more sense than the script. I almost liked the eye fucking scene but I think that was more reflex than anything else.

I learned a couple of weeks ago that adult, male chimpanzees like nothing so much as to pop open a brew and watch a very violent movie on TV. The chimps bark and scream, they throw punches at the air and jump up and down on their seats. Chimps love violence. Everybody loves violence.

I even like the violence on *Sons of Anarchy*, though that violence is pathetic. The fights on the show are like watching drag queens slap at each other. I never cringe or clench my fists but I will still watch the violent parts of this show anyway, because deep, down inside I am an adult, male chimpanzee. And, a silly fight is better than no fight.

Unfortunately, the fights are less than the arguments. And, the arguments are less than the soul searching. *Sons of Anarchy* suffers from what Clint Eastwood once called, "Too much talk, talk. Not enough bang, bang."

"Crappy office. Cops. Cops in this town are really a bunch of little bitches. This motorcycle club is lucky it isn't in Torrance. More estrogen chat. Girls jog. No jiggle. Katey Sagal gives Jax's girlfriend a bloody nose. Hey! Where is Drea DeMatteo? Isn't she in this show anymore? Jax visits bitch cop. 'People die! People

225

get hurt!' What are you talking about Jax? Don't talk about it. Be about it. 'That was not on me," some guy says. Must stay awake.

"Amateur video surveillance of an arson. No chain of custody. Who gives a crap? Henry Rollins is a thug for the real estate developers who wear suits! Why do they need a thug? Don't they have lawyers? Did he accidentally spray deodorant in his mouth for a real long time? Is that why he has that look on his face? More girl talk. 'I know what it's like to keep something like this inside.' Blah, blah, blah. This is more boring than a Jay Dobyns interview."

The reason for all the talk, I am guessing, is that the one and only character in this show is an institution called the *Sons of Anarchy* Motorcycle Club. All the actual people in the show are just there so the wardrobe dressers will have something to hang the cuts on. And, the character which is the club, is just a kid's collection of clichés.

I can see that Sutter obviously wants to be sympathetic to this subculture. Because he is a romantic or he is an egomaniac or because he is having a mid-life crisis or for whatever reason Sutter wants to be our storyteller telling "our soap opera."

And that, I think is an admirable goal. Kudos Kurt! Kudos! Bravo! Bravo for your intentions! Why doesn't everybody just take a moment to clap right now. For Kurt. Before I give him more notes.

Kurt, one problem, the least problem, you might have of realizing your beautiful dream is that you are like the man who decides he is qualified to moralize about the working conditions in the handkerchief industry because he blew his nose. That is the minor problem.

The more serious problem is that Sutter is a writer who suffers from delusions of adequacy.

Stories worth telling or hearing are never about institutions like motorcycle clubs, or *The West Wing* or *NCIS Fargo*. *Sons of Anarchy* is a title, not a character. (Yeah, I know that the lead character in *The Shining* was a haunted hotel but I don't think anybody will ever confuse Sutter with Stanley Kubrick.) Except when told by a genius, all stories have always been about people, even if, as in *Uncle Remus*, the people are wearing bunny suits. The problem with *Sons of Anarchy* is that the people have to wear costumes so you can tell who and what they are. In Sons of Anarchy, there is nobody inside the bunny suit.

That is ironic because the most interesting people in the world are bikers. Sutter has the budget to make a weekly television show about this terrific subject with all these fascinating characters and the best he can come up with is something that aspires to be *General Hospital*.

An obvious impediment to reaching the lofty standards of *As The Biker World Turns* is that the show got off to a bad start. All stories must always start the same way: The hero has a serious problem.

In the case of *Sons of Anarchy* the hero is a young man named Jax. And, his serious problem is that he has an identity crisis. Jax finds a book his father wrote that disillusions him about his life as a motorcycle outlaw in general and his club in particular. And, you don't need to be a writer to understand that this is pathetically weak. Worst of all, Sutter compounded this error by never throwing that first piece of paper away. Over and over he seems to keep trying to make this ridiculous premise work.

This secret book (in Hollywood development circles it is a pseudo-intellectual convention called "the secret knowledge") is supposed to personify Jax's father's ghost. And, because of this we are supposed to connect *Sons of Anarchy* to Shakespeare's play *Hamlet*.

227

And, I hardly know what more to say about that. I have tried before. I will fail again now. The first obvious thing that sputters out this time is that the play *Hamlet* was named for a character. It wasn't named the *Danish National Racket*. And secondly, *Hamlet* isn't about a young man being haunted by his father's ghost. *Hamlet* is about revenge. Not haunting. Revenge.

I wake up many mornings motivated by revenge. Personally. I enjoy breaking laws for those times when the law has tried to break me. I want my life that I should have had instead of the one I got. And I want revenge on the sons of bitches who stole what I should have had from me. Everywhere I look I see revenge. Mongols want revenge on Angels. Angels want revenge on Outlaws. And, everybody hates the police.

The real world that Sutter has decided to dramatize is full of rage, disappointment, affliction, jealousy, shame and lust. The biker subculture is at least the most interesting thing in America. The men are flawed, complex and capable. The women are tough, long suffering and sexually manipulative.

This is William James "Moral Equivalent of War." This is an angry and ironic subculture. This is the world of the disposed working class. This is a subculture full of character motivation. People will fight one another just because it is a red moon. But when Sutter writes a fight scene that fight is no more angry than a studio lunch. He never writes the anger. He only writes the punch.

Sutter never sees a man drowning his sorrows. Sutter sees a drunk. Occasionally Sutter shows men riding motorcycles but he doesn't seem to have any idea why anyone would ride let alone run. Mostly he shows men parking motorcycles. Because why not? It is easier to pose when the bike is standing still.

"Every character nuance, every detail is not wasted," Sutter wrote the other day. What character nuance? What character? After a year of trying, I am still not sophisticated enough to "plug in."

But back to the notes:

"Sons hang out in a barber shop? With a sheriff who is getting a shave? What is this? Deadwood? Didn't that guy used to be on Deadwood? Fight! Henry Rollins knocks over a bike. And, they let him get away with that? No knives? No breaker bars? Voice over narration sounds like dramatic reading of the memoirs of Swiss Depth Psychologist Carl Jung. Maybe next they will eat some shrooms and meet a flying mandala that will lead them to an all knowing coyote. Katey Sagal was beaten and raped? When did this happen? A month ago?! And she doesn't want to tell anybody. Because she 'didn't want to twist up the club.' What? I am lost.

"Charlie Hunnum and girl have gloomy chat. 'My Dad wrote this. His vision for the club. What went wrong and how to save it.' What the fuck is he talking about? What is wrong with the club? You mean like some fucking guy can knock over your motorcycle without getting hit in the knees with a breaker bar? Wrong like that? Chapter church. Godfather bullshit. Is that a Holdem table? 'Retaliation must be harsh and immediate. That's what we do.' They are talking about Otto getting eye fucked. Not the bike. Blah, blah, blah. 'We gotta wait.' What? Why? What a bunch of pussies these guys are. Slow motion scene. Mumbles. 'We gotta protect this club?' What? Is it a motorcycle club or a development deal? More grim mumbles. Why is it so dark? Didn't these guys pay their electric bill?

"Tender moment between Katey Sagal and Ron Perlman. Mumbles. Anguished looks. Nobody laughs. Big hugs. Minivan blows up in slow motion. Not like things blow up for real but like a distant napalm strike in a war movie directed by a draft dodger. Somebody says 'Oh my God.' I don't know why. Guy gets knocked out. He's alright. He is not bleeding from his

229

ears, nose or eyes. He's alright. How come nobody is laughing at him? When I get knocked out, when I wake up people are laughing at me."

And, then what? I don't know. This seems to be a show where nothing happens and when something happens it does not matter. There never seems to be an "and then."

The way stories, as most people understand that word, work is that somebody has a problem and in fixing that problem he creates another, unexpected problem and that leads to another complication and so on and so on. All of that action together makes a narrative. But Sutter must be after something more sophisticated than mere narrative.

Sophisticated. Like what?

Well everybody, *tout le monde*, agrees that the most sophisticated story ever written is Samuel Beckett's late 1940s play *Waiting For Godot*. It was written in French and correctly titled *En attendant Godot*. Of course it was written in French. It had to be written in French. I am guessing that Sutter read or saw or acted in *Godot* while he was getting his Master of Fine Arts degree from Northern Illinois University a few years ago.

The action of the play is two guys sitting on a bench waiting for someone named Godot. One of the two characters can barely speak. The mumbling small talk goes on for two acts. Godot never shows up. At one point the two men on a bench contemplate hanging themselves but eventually decide to do nothing because "it is safer." Doing nothing is always safer. Sitting on the motorcycle while it is parked is always safer than sitting on the motorcycle while it moves.

I know about this because a woman made me go see *Waiting For Godot*. She was pretty good but she wasn't worth it. Seven women all in one big pile for a week might have been worth it. But she was only one woman and as it turned out it was only one night.

In fact, I think *Waiting For Godot* is probably the second most boring thing I have ever seen. But, back to my notes.

"Why isn't anybody trying to wake this guy up? Is he supposed to be dead? It wasn't that big an explosion. There isn't even a crater. There wasn't any debris. Is he dead? I wonder what his name was? Roll end credits. Thank God that is finally over. That was the most boring thing I've ever seen. That was worse than *Waiting For Godot.*"

I call out to my woman. "Hey Baby? Hey sweetheart? Would you do me a big favor? Would you call up six of your friends and ask them to come over here for about a week?"

Neither the man nor the woman move.

"Well, then, hey baby? Would you make me some jambalaya?"

They do not move.

Baby, would you make me a hot dog?"

No one moves.

"Well, will you at least get me a bottle of beer?

Still they do not move.

See Kurt. I can do it, too.

The Hemet Hoax

In 1954 a satirist named Leonard Wibberley wrote a six part serial for the *Saturday Evening Post* magazine called "The Day New York Was Invaded." The next year the story was published by Little, Brown and Company with a title most people recognize, *The Mouse That Roared.* The comedy became a Peter Sellers movie four years after that. It failed as a television series in 1963 but was successfully produced as a play. The play is still an amateur theater standard. It will probably half fill some high school auditorium somewhere this year.

The Mouse That Roared is about a tiny, backward and insignificant European Country called the Duchy of Grand Fenwick that declares war on the United States. Grand Fenwick expects to quickly lose and then apply for the same sort of American foreign aid the United States bestowed on Japan and Germany after World War II.

Grand Fenwick must lose. It does not want to win. Its army wears chain mail and is armed with bows and arrows. All it wants is the money. Unfortunately the prank takes off in unexpected directions. The United States does not notice the invasion for two months.

Then officials mistake the medieval Fenwickians for space aliens.

I keep waiting for somebody to call the city of Hemet, California the Duchy of Grand Fenwick. So far no one else has so I will. Hemet is the Duchy of Grand Fenwick.

The plucky, little, Hemet Police Department is now at war with and under siege by the by the big, bad Vagos Motorcycle Club. Right this minute an agent in Beverly Hills is pitching this farce as "*The Mouse That Roared* meets *The Wild One*." Clint Eastwood should play the police chief. The principal Vagos should be Shrek, the Hulk and Kermit the Frog. The happy ending will come when Hemet learns it has finally won that big pile of federal money and its police force has been saved.

Okay, probably the movie will fail. The great, Hemet motorcycle club war has already proven that the greater part of modern policing is theatrical performance. So a movie would just be superfluous. And, even if the movie was made nobody would laugh. The other thing the Hemet hoax proves is that in the last fifty years America has become a lot more stupid and a lot less fun.

Fifty years ago a cynical press would have instantly recognized that someone in Riverside County, on behalf of the Hemet Police, has made this whole Hemet story up. The story was invented because the Hemet Police really want the money. Because Hemet has been hit particularly hard by the ongoing sequel to the Great Depression. And, keeping the peace has become an extravagant, insane cargo cult. The worth of modern police forces is now measured by how much money a department can get and spend on symbols of policing.

The current Hemet Police Chief is Richard Dana. Dana looks and sounds a lot like Clint Eastwood. He put on a badge in 1965. He took the Hemet job when he was 62. He replaced a man named Pete Hewitt who retired from the job at 61. Dana took the job because he "can't imagine doing anything else." And, also the job pays $163,000 a year. So besides pursuing his passion for goodness and justice Dana also gets to put a few dollars in his pocket. In his mid-sixties Dana still looks like a leading man. He might be able to stay on the job for another ten years, for another million and a half dollars. And, he is about to enter the fourth year of a five year contract.

When he took the job Dana's supporters anticipated that he would be "growing" the Hemet Police Department. He was actually able to grow the force to 93 officers. The housing bubble made Hemet, which has about 70,000 residents, look like a budding metropolis. Then the Hemet of the future turned out to be just another illusion in a long con. The Los Angeles *Times* describes the city as "foreclosure-stricken." Sales tax revenue dropped 27 percent in the first two months of 2009. During Dana's administration the police force has declined to 68 officers.

The depression has left Hemet and Dana to fend largely for themselves. As part of the Economic Stimulus Package the Obama Administration promised $1 billion to keep cops employed. But nationally police forces applied for $8.3 billion to offset police layoffs. Hemet had to compete with all those other police departments in big mean cities like Oakland and Detroit for money. And, it probably did not help Hemet's cause that crime in the city actually declined ten percent from 2007 to 2008.

Hemet applied for and did not get a $312,000 federal grant for traffic enforcement. The city also sought a $772,000 grant to pay for its police force and got less than half that amount. The police department also got a $213,000 grant to buy new computers and dispatch equipment but Hemet was forbidden to use the money to pay cops.

About a year ago the Hemet SWAT – of course Hemet has a "Special Operations Unit" – bought a $270,000 armored vehicle called a BearCat with a grant from the Department of Homeland Security. But again the money could not be used to pay for cop's salaries. The money had to be used for an armored car.

Hemet invested, as many foundering police departments have, in the red light camera racket. The reason why these cameras are a racket is because they do not do what they are advertised to do and they make insiders rich by preying on innocuous citizens. Almost all of the infractions these robots ticket are for a rolling stop when a motorist makes a right turn on red.

Last summer, on Dana's recommendation, Hemet signed a contract with a company named Nestor Traffic Systems. Nestor was in bankruptcy at the time. The penalty for a right turn on red after a rolling stop in Hemet was set at $446 and the city guaranteed Nestor Traffic Systems $60,000 a month. Anything more than $720,000 dollars a year, which works out to about 1,600 tickets, will be gravy for Hemet. So if the ticket robots issue a mere 9,100 tickets a year Dana can get his force back up to 93 officers. A study of the busiest intersection in Hemet discovered around 1,600 rolling stop right turns on red in a single day. So it seemed very feasible that the Hemet Police might be saved by robot red light cameras.

Alas, by last fall Hemet was running about $800,000 in the red. Several radicals suggested that Hemet fire its entire police force and contract out the job of policing Hemet to another agency like the Riverside County Sheriff's Department. The situation had degenerated that far. People had begun to ask unthinkable questions. Did Sheriff Andy make $163,000 a year. Did Mayberry have a BearCat? A Swat team? How much did Barney Fife make? People began to ask rude, despicable, naïve, uninformed, stupid, sarcastic questions like that.

City Manager Len Wood, who was sitting next to Chief Dana at the time by the way, explained at a "roundtable:"

"I just don't think that (contracting out police services) is a viable option. My experience includes contracting and full service. I found that while initially there might be some saving from contracting, what usually happens and what does happen is you lose control of how you set your rates. What generally happens is, whether it's the county or whatever, they set the rates, they set the salary levels, they set the retirement levels and you're going to pay for it. If the contract is cheaper, it usually means the service level has suffered considerably.

"The current state of the economy has put many police forces on the defensive. Thoughtful people of disparate political philosophies have questions why America needs so many police investigating and prosecuting so many people, why the police must be so elaborately militarized and technologically equipped and what will result from America imprisoning a higher percentage of its citizens than any other nation in the world."

Fortunately for Hemet, this is an interesting time in human evolution when people's understanding of life and the world around them is shaped at least as much by mass media as by direct, actual experience. Mass media are also, for the most part, self-perpetuating, profit seeking, competitive businesses. And, in the two decades since *Cops* and *America's Most Wanted* both debuted on *Fox* a symbiotic relationship has grown like a cancer connecting the mass media business to the police business.

A media critic named Colin Gunckel has named this weird development "Gangs Gone Wild." Gunckel uses the phrase to describe one way conventional journalism has "begun to compete with and incorporate the conventions of reality programming."

More and more, police get praise and cash for attracting media attention. As the world becomes increasingly "post-literate" the line between *Sons of Anarchy*, *Gangland*, *America Most Wanted*, *TMZ*, the *Associated Press* and the Los Angeles *Times* grows ever fainter. Unless you live in a cardboard box you know that an ever more hysterical, mass-media fueled panic about safety and crime has been growing for years. And, even if you do live in a cardboard box you must have noticed that policing everywhere has become increasingly "performative" – a word coined by social scientists to describe how the mundane behavior of ordinary people has begun to mimic the behavior of Heidi and Spencer and Snooki and Tha Situation on *MTV*.

The cops are not immune to the social forces that buffet everyone else. Some police agencies, like the ATF, are very sophisticated about mass media. And, even if people are much stupider than they once were there will still pause to read the alarming phrases "Terrorist Threat" and "Outlaw Motorcycle Gang."

There is always federal money to fight terrorism and gangs. Especially for smart, old cops who get how the world really works now. Much, but hardly all, of the money comes from a federal program called COPS. COPS is an acronym for Community Oriented Policing Services. According to its web site: "The COPS Office serves a noble purpose. In alignment with our component partners within the Department of Justice, our mission is to create safer communities across this country through the advancement of community policing.

"Community Policing, in its simplest terms, is about building relationships and solving problems. Our Office strives to make it possible for Police Chiefs and Sheriffs across the country to achieve these objectives in the most effective manner possible, consistent with their local requirements."

And really, what could be a nobler than trying to save a town that is being overrun by menacing outlaw bikers? Policing in Hemet in general has become more performative as the survival of the department has become more tenuous. If people are going to be so rude as to ask why Hemet needs a police department then the Hemet police are left with no choice but to show them.

Last June, Hemet lost three police sergeants, a detective and two officers. And later that same month, a regional gang task force announced the arrests of 16 adults and one juvenile during a gang "sweep operation" of the Hemet-San Jacinto area. "We target violent gangs every day in the city of Hemet," Dana said in his press release. "But today we gave them a little extra attention. The regional gang task forces are very effective in their communities, but when we bring them together like this, they are able to strike multiple targets at once. It's impressive and effective. The citizens win and the bad guys lose when we pool our resources."

In just the last month Hemet has absurdly over-reacted to a couple of "possible terrorist threats."

On February 22 a Filipino immigrant left a suitcase at the federal building in Hemet that houses the Social Security Administration and Immigration and Customs Enforcement. Hemet cops evacuated the building, detonated the suitcase, and took the disgruntled man into custody. It was categorized as a bomb threat although there was never any bomb.

Just last Thursday, as Chief Dana was trumpeting another threat, police closed much of downtown Hemet because a homeless woman had abandoned two empty suitcases. She later claimed the cases were not hers after police destroyed them with a water cannon. The remote controlled destruction of the two empty suitcases was supervised by a "hazardous materials team."

All of this is the context in which Hemet police and the Riverside County District Attorney announced the arrest last Wednesday, Saint Patrick's Day, of at least 30 members of the Vagos Motorcycle Club.

Riverside (California) County District Attorney Rod Pacheco called a press conference to announce that some unknown number of police, but more than 400, from more than "sixty local and federal police agencies" raided 94 locations in four states. Pacheco and Chief Dana, who also attended the media event, both implied in the strongest possible way that the raids were retaliation for a series of attacks on police in Hemet by the Vagos.

Pacheco even gave the purported series of raids an ATF style name. He called them "Operation Everywhere." But unlike most large scale, multi-agency police operations, neither Pacheco nor Dana nor anyone else has ever produced an indictment, a list of departments involved, a list of arrestees or an elaboration of the crimes with which they have been charged. The details of "Operation Everywhere" are like Joe McCarthy's list of hundreds of known communists in the State Department. The details are a piece of paper to be waved around in plain sight but never read.

Last New Year's Eve somebody improvised a way to fill the "Hemet/San Jacinto Valley Gang Task Force" headquarters with natural gas. It was very smelly. Somebody was forced to find a wrench, turn off the gas, and let the building air out. The more time that passed the more dramatically this "deliberate act" has been described. Last week a Hemet cop described it as an attempt to take "out half a city block." In February a zip gun was attached to a black steel gate. When a cop opened the gate the zip gun fired. The more days pass the closer the small caliber bullet is said to have come to the cop's head. On March 5, somebody attached an explosive device, presumably a pipe bomb, to another cop's car.

The fact that neither Pacheco or Dana would actually come out and say that the Vagos were attacking police in Hemet only emphasized the mendacity of both these men and the hoax they have perpetrated for their own cynical gain. Pacheco and Dana just stood next to a table covered with Vagos paraphernalia and insisted that the press draw its own conclusions. The press has been more than willing to oblige.

That almost everything Pacheco and Dana said at the news conference was an obvious lie has gone unreported. The story continues to run. Yesterday the story was advanced by "news" that a threat to bomb "a police vehicle in retaliation for the Vagos arrests" had been phoned into Hemet Police headquarters. Saturday night, television reporters in Los Angeles were still reporting this story at the top of the news and doing their "stand-ups" outside a dramatically fortified Hemet Police Department.

Thomas Watkins, who is flamboyantly and incompetently covering the story for *The Associated Press*, reported the other day that, "Investigators are trying to determine what may have prompted an outlaw motorcycle gang to set three booby traps on gang enforcement officers in Riverside County." Watkins does not hesitate to report as fact that the Vagos have gone to war with Hemet. He goes on to report that, "one theory is that members of the Vagos gang could

240

have been affronted when a gang enforcement unit in Hemet monitored their group as they attended a funeral."

Sure. Or maybe the Hemet Police Department is just looking for some attention and some money.

Sunday morning this story ran in China.

And, the *AP* was reporting, "The tense atmosphere surrounding a California police department plagued by booby trap attacks has been stepped up a notch following the latest threat against officers... About 30 members of the Vagos, California's largest motorcycle gang, were arrested in Riverside County on Wednesday, as part of a crackdown across the state and in Arizona, Nevada and Utah. The gang specializes in methamphetamine sales, identity theft and violence...Dana said someone he believes may have been a gang member tried to get into a news conference Thursday at the district attorney's office in Riverside. The person was turned away, he said, because he didn't have a press credential."

Heaven forbid any outsider should get into the press conference. That might mark the end of the world. Better to let the real pros like Tom Watkins cover this stinking, heaping pile of news product.

Sunday morning this story was being headlined: "The evolution of crime: Urban terrorism." That angle on the story was coined by Jerry Brown, who is one of the three multi-millionaires in the running to become the next Governor of California.

"It is incredible and even unprecedented for police officers here to be subject to terrorist attack," Brown said at the news conference which skeptical journalists were forbidden to attend.. "We have seen it south of the border, but not here yet."

Hemet hasn't gotten its money yet but it has already gotten more attention than the Duchy of Grand Fenwick ever did. So far this phony news story manufactured on behalf of the money hungry Hemet Police Department seems to have made a pretty good start.

The only real question is how long news coverage of this absurd hoax is going to go on.

Watching Lindeman Die

I perch on the on the edge of a classic 80s coffee table in a classic 70s living room. I stare without blinking at a modern, 30 inch television screen. And for the six hundredth, or eight hundredth or thousandth, or fifteen hundredth time, I watch John Lindeman die.

I don't know how many times I have seen Lindeman die. Go out into the Mojave on a new moon night. Look up at the sky. Count the stars. Probably, I have seen Lindeman die about that many times.

John Curtis Unterseher "Ripley" Lindeman was 43 and Bradley Burritt Lutzow was 45 when they were murdered last February 17 outside a QuikTrip convenience store near 19th and Peoria Avenues in Phoenix, Arizona. Lutzow was from Durand, Illinois. Lindeman lived in Golden Valley, Arizona. Both men belonged to a clean and sober motorcycle club called the Association of Recovering Motorcyclists (A.R.M.) I have been told countless times that they were murdered by members of the Sober Riders Motorcycle Club because the Sober Riders claim Arizona.

Both clubs describe themselves as self-help groups. Neither club wears a bottom or side rocker. Neither club wears a one percent patch.

The Sober Riders are alleged to be the "largest clean and sober motorcycle club in the United States." And it continues to be a prominent club in Arizona. The club's one piece patch was easy to spot at the Third Annual Riot on the River Run on the weekend of October 9. A week later the club's "Casa Grande Crew" co-hosted a motorcycle rodeo with the Red and Black. November 28th in Phoenix, the club will sponsor its Fifth Annual "Takin' It To The Streets" run. If the club has made enemies, it seems not to have made enemies who shoot back.

The Sober Riders Motorcycle Club was founded in 1994 by a man named Pat "Pooh Bear" Conley. In his most widely circulated photograph, Conley appears to be a right, jolly, old elf. He is still President of the Sober Riders. For at least a half dozen years he was the President of the Arizona Confederation of Motorcycle Clubs. And, although he has stepped down from that post he still contributes a column to the Confederation's newsletter, the *Arizona Spokesman*.

In last May's *Spokesman*, three months after Lindeman and Lutzow were assassinated, Conley contributed a touching anecdote that he seems to have invented to demonstrate his wisdom and good will. His theme was that all motorcycle clubs should just get along.

"Recently at a run attended by many new clubs," Conley began, "as indicated by so many new and different patches, a bystander asked an old gray bearded member of an older well established club.

"'How do you feel about all these new clubs?'

"The Old Gray Beard replied, 'it is good, the more the better for our cause.'

"'Your cause?' asked the bystander.

"'Not my cause. Our cause. Our rights. Our liberty, Our freedom. All the things held dear to us all! Our cause includes you as an independent and Patch Holders alike.'

"'Wow! How do you all get along with so many different opinions as signified by so many different clubs?' asked the slick back.

"'We treat each other not as we wish to be treated, but as the other guy wishes to be treated. It is simple courtesy,' replied the Patch Holder. All this brought to mind the movie *Pay it Forward.*"

Conley wrote this self-serving homily, including his apparently unintentionally ironic reference to the Buddhist concept of *karma*, well after, according to multiple trusted sources, he sat in a Denny's restaurant in Phoenix and told Lindeman (who had lived in Arizona for years and was employed by a newspaper named the Arizona *Republic*) to get out of the state.

(One second hand but cogent source has described Conley's ultimatum as very blunt and unequivocal. Conley, of course is presumed innocent until proven guilty in a court of law. I am just trying to tell a story, is all. You can believe anything you want.)

While preparing this story I wrote Conley and asked him for his side.

"Dear Mr. Conley," I wrote. "This is your chance to influence what I write. At your request, anything you do not want attributed to you will not be. I protect sources. If you just ignore me, I will identify you by name as having stonewalled me. You can answer the questions you are comfortable answering and ignore the others. No problem. But I will notice which ones you answer and which ones you don't. I really think that most of these questions are softballs."

Among the questions I asked Conley were:

"Were you at the sit down that preceded the murders? Did you give the A.R.M. representatives an ultimatum to stay out of Arizona? Do you have a version of that meeting?"

"As far as you are concerned, are members of the Association of Recovering Motorcyclists welcome to fly their patch in Arizona?"

"Has the SRMC been inaccurately characterized by me or by anyone else? Tell me how."

Conley stonewalled me.

The first time I look at the video of Lindeman dying I can hardly see anything. I write down questions. Who is that? What did he say? When is this? The first time I look I see the dark shadow of Lindeman die forty or fifty times. The next day I watch him die five or six times. I am very stupid so it is not until about day three that I start playing with the brightness and contrast and color saturation.

Frankly, I prefer not to watch Ripley Lindeman die. So I try that for a week. But when I don't look I feel guilty. So then I look another 20 or 30 times.

And, life goes on. The world persists with or without us. I measure out my days with scribbles in boxes on a calendar. Then I turn a page and scribble some more. Before I know it I have been watching Lindeman die for months.

It is not exactly a secret that I have a copy of this video. A week or so ago, a relative of one of the victims asked me to post the video on this site. I promised I would give it a shot. I promised that if not the video, I would at least post a few words. And, I promised that knowing that my words, these words, are a poor substitute for letting you see Lindeman die with your own eyes. "Give me until Monday," I said.

The problem is, the legally obtained video I watch has its own little history. It has made a journey through several hands. And, among the scars it wears is that along the way it has been converted to .WMV format, which means that it contains a single digit percentage of the information the original video had. Before I could analyze the video I watch in any meaningful way I had to up convert it into .AVI format. That up conversion, however, did not really increase the information on the video, only the number of pixels. And, after days of fiddling I had to concede that even if I posted the video, no one would really be able to see anything. All you could see is what I told you I saw anyway.

I give a copy of the video to someone who knows how to enhance these things in various, clever ways. He grabbed dozens of frames for me. I play with the frames in Photoshop. I take notes.

By Saturday afternoon, Halloween, I have been watching the video for four days straight. I cannot show you what I have seen so I am stuck with the task of describing what I have seen. I can do that, I decide. I do this stuff all the time.

In fact, I already have this story outlined in my mind. The outline goes:

- The video is one minute and nine seconds long.
- John Lindeman strides into the QuikTrip twelve seconds into the video.
- At forty two seconds, just outside the front door, John Lindeman dies. He dies. I know he dies. I have seen men die. So, I recognize that Lindeman has died. Even if I had not seen men die I would see that Ripley Lindeman died beautifully. He died beautifully as the Loyalist Militiaman died beautifully in Robert Capa's classic photograph, "The Falling Soldier:" Falling, spinning, elegant, brave, poetically doomed. Except Capa's photograph was a fraud and Lindeman really died. What I

247

cannot tell is whether Lindeman died after he hit the ground or before.

- As Lindeman dies a clerk in the QuikTrip says, "Damn!" The clerk utters that curse three times between second 12 and second 42 of the video. "Damn bro...damn...Damn!" The clerk says that third "damn" the way Martin Lawrence used to say "damn" when he would look at his girlfriend's ass: Damn spelled with a gratuitous number of aitches. "Dahhhhhmn!"

I look it up. The common, English, four letter word damn is derived from either the Latin *damnare*, to condemn. Or from the Greek *daptein*, to devour. Or from the Old Norse *tafn*, to make a human sacrifice. Take your pick. I think the clerk is describing all three of the above.

The clerk says "damn" as in, "Dahhmn, girl! You sure look fine!" Normally, listening to a convenience store clerk say "Dahhmn!" about a thousand or two thousand times would get on my nerves. But I can also hear the awe and fear in the clerk's voice. He isn't a clerk saying "damn." He is a frightened dog barking at a ghost in the night.

The clerk says "damn" as Lindeman dies.

There were three members of A.R.M. at the QuikTrip that night: Lindeman, Lutzow and a third man who has never been named. The third man drove the dying Lutzow to a nearby hospital. For months, I assumed that Lindeman and Lutzow were killed side by side while the surviving member of A.R.M. waited in the truck. And, that after the shooting the survivor checked on both men and dragged or fireman-carried the still breathing Lutzow off to the truck and then drove him to the hospital. Watching the video tears that conjecture apart.

248

As my copy of the video starts, the first witness, a white man wearing a blue tee shirt and a gray baseball cap walks into the store reaching into his back pocket. This first witness takes twelve, easy strides then disappears out of the left side of the frame. Just barely visible through the front left window is John Lindeman, wearing a denim jacket over a dark sweatshirt and a baseball cap. On the video the cap looks like a beanie but when the frame is grabbed and enhanced it becomes a blue or black baseball cap with a tan bill. Lindeman is pacing around in a pair of heavy, dark work boots. Maybe he smells the coming storm of violence. He obviously has no idea that storm will break as soon as it does.

Six seconds into the video, someone approaches Lindeman from the direction of the gas pumps. For five or six or seven hundred times I think this must be Brad Lutzow but I eventually start to think of him as "The Fighter" and I begin to suspect he is the A.R.M who lived.

"The Fighter" takes Lindeman's place, standing watch next to the front door and at eleven seconds, the second witness, a portly white man in a maroon tee shirt and wearing white sneakers opens the stage right front door. Simultaneously, Lindeman opens the other front door and politely lets the man in the maroon shirt enter first. As the second witness enters he, in turn, politely steps aside and holds open his door for the third and fourth witnesses, two, young, possibly Hispanic men in hoodies and baggy pants.

Witnesses three and four clear the front door when Lindeman is seven steps into the store. Lindeman walks with the slightly stiff shoulders of a man who does bench presses but other than that he seems relaxed, unremarkable and oblivious to the approaching danger ten or twelve yards behind his back.

Before the fourth witness clears the front door, in full sight of the fifth witness, the store clerk, three men trace Lindeman's steps across the parking lot from the gas pumps. They appear out of the gloom, behind the glare of the front door glass, like ghosts.

I think one of them looks like a troll and that is how I start to think of him. He is a stocky, bearded man wearing a light colored bandana and a denim vest over a black, leather jacket. He was born to be a villain. The way he walks is obnoxious. He is looking for a fight. When he stops in front of the Fighter his knees are a little bent and he is leaning aggressively forward so that his arms look longer and more simian than they probably are.

I have been told by someone with knowledge of the fight that this actor is the leader of the Sober Riders war party. I have heard three versions of what he said as he exited a white, crew-cab pick up truck. The versions are practically identical. They differ principally in punctuation, inflection and the inclusion or exclusion of the word "mother." What I think he said was, "Where's the little fucker?" And, I have inferred from this that the attack was premeditated; that the first thing the Sober Riders did when they arrived was acquire the location of their targets, and the target who was John Lindeman was already inside the store and so he was out of sight.

Can you hear it now? "Where's the LITTLE fucker?"

The same day I wrote to Pooh Bear Conley I also wrote to Matthew Verthein, the detective who may or may not still be investigating this case. I sent him a list of 16 questions. And, with all the subtlety I can manage, which is not much, I ask him about the stocky, bearded man wearing the bandanna. But, first I ask Verthein:

"Is the investigation still active? No bullshit, okay. How does a case get classified as cold? What

250

happens when a case is classified as cold? What is the murder clearance rate in Phoenix?"

I know the national clearance rate on murders is around 61 percent. I know that most of the murders that are solved are something like when a husband murders his wife. I think the Sober Murders might not be a "Who done it." But these murders are pretty surely a "How To Prove It."

To his credit, Verthein does not stone wall me. He replies:

"It would be highly inappropriate and unprofessional to share information with you in a confidential manner. That would not be fair to the victims families as well as others who have made public records requests."

Really, if I had known his response in advance I might have just gone ahead asked him to make me a photocopy of the case book. But he will not even tell me if the case is active or cold. So I am stuck with reading between the lines. My best guess is that Verthein is still investigating.

And, I also suspect he is stumped because the next thing he writes is: "From your questions it appears to me you may have information that may be helpful to this investigation. If you want to meet with me, call me, or share what you know anonymously, I am open to a meeting, a phone call, or you can contact our Silent Witness program and remain anonymous."

Verthein may have missed the part when I explained that: "*The Aging Rebel* does not cooperate with the police. *The Aging Rebel* sympathizes with the survivors of the victims and with the fugitive suspects equally."

Verthein asks me to give him a drink. And, if he is asking me for water I think his well must be going dry.

I have been told the same three names for months: Spike, Orphan and Sly. And, I have also been told that the Sober Rider who looks like a troll is called Sly.

The troll-like Sober Rider is followed across the lot by two other Sober Riders. When he stops they flank him. They are taller than the Troll. The three of them stop about ten feet from The Fighter who is standing against the front of the building. The Troll smirks and appears to say something. I leave open the possibility that this is when he asks, "Where's the little fucker?"

The Fighter straightens up, takes four steps and hits the Troll with a big, straight right on the left side of his chin. It is a very nice punch. The first thousand times I saw it I almost cheered. It is the kind of punch you try to teach your kid to throw. You can hear it land on the audio inside the store. And, the Troll was unmistakably asking for it.

I have been told by confident sources that the A.R.M. started it. Maybe this is what they are talking about. I back up the tape. Look again. Take notes.

The Troll stops right in front of the QuikTrip door and spreads his legs 19 seconds into the video. The Fighter punches the Troll in the face at second 21. The Troll rocks back a foot. His knees buckle and he is sitting on his backside at second 22. He would have gone flat on his back except that a fourth Sober Rider has hurried over to catch him. You can hear the clatter he makes when he falls.

There are not just three Sober Riders. There are more than four. My best guess is that there are nine.

The Fighter still has two more Sober Riders to fend off. Through the front window, next to the candy bars, you can see one combatant backing another up with slow, heavy jabs. The fight has a cinematic flair.

At the clattering sound John Lindeman jogs toward the door. Near the cash register he breaks into a sprint. By 27 seconds into the video Lindeman is out the door and he has 15 seconds to live.

There may be the sound of a gunshot at around 27 seconds. If it is a gunshot it is coming from over by the gas pumps, where I think Brad Lutzow has just texted his wife in Illinois, "I love you."

By the time Lindeman is out the door there are clearly two fights going on. The one that is all but impossible to see on the video I have is the fight near the gas pumps. I suspect that Brad Lutzow, whether he has already been shot or not, is in the middle of that one. Lindeman hesitates for a fraction of a second then runs off to the pumps.

By then, the Troll has managed to find his feet and he has grabbed the Fighter from behind. He holds the Fighter's arms behind his back so the other Sober Riders can get their punches in. Eventually, the Fighter flings the Troll off but by then the Fighter is already going down.

At 29 seconds the clerk says, "Damn, bro!"

In the background, outside, somebody is yelling "Huh! Huh! Huh," like a martial artist breaking boards. It might be someone throwing kicks and punches. A second-hand source has also told me that the sound I hear is the sound of one of the combatants striking another with a collapsible baton.

There is a sharp report which may be a gun shot deep in the parking lot at 31 seconds. The clerk says "Damn" again. The shot seems to come from the direction of the gas pumps. I think it is probably the shot that killed Brad Lutzow. Then somebody honks their horn from second 33 to second 34. And, a car hurriedly backs out into the street trying to escape. Another second hand source has told me that the headlights I see belong to a car driven by a Sober Rider. The headlights are where they are because the Sober

Riders have blocked the driveway. And now, the Sober Riders have begun their escape.

At 36 seconds, someone rises and appears in the front window of the convenience store. I suspect it is the surviving member of A.R.M. the guy I think of as the fighter. He rises and appears ready to head into the parking lot in the direction of the disappearing headlights of the fleeing car.

Two unmistakable gun shots ring out at second 37 and the man who has risen seems ready to head toward them. The shots are getting closer to the microphone. At second 38 another shot rings out and the man who is undecided about entering the parking lot turns and runs.

Then the fight finds its climax.

The gunshot at second 40 of the tape is the loudest so far. As the shot sounds you can see John Lindeman running straight at one of the Sober Riders.

Lindeman is running with his hands out in front of him as if he is trying to avenge Lutzow, as if he can't wait to get his hands around his adversaries throat. You can see the shots hit him. One shot hardly slows him down. Another shot makes his back arch. His hands fly up in the classic pose of a man who has been shot. But he keeps coming. The gunman fires three times while running backward. At the third shot Lindeman falls at his killers feet, just outside the door of the QuikTrip. The killer lifts his left foot so Lindeman will not fall on him. It is the move a toreador makes as he elegantly evades a bull. You can hear Lindeman hit the ground. The way he falls, you can see he is dead.

And, inside the store the clerk says, "Dahhhhmn!" As if this is the best movie or the worst movie he has ever seen.

The killer strides away. He stops to pick something up. The first thousand times I watch the video I think it is probably a spent cartridge. And, I wonder if the killer bent to pick this thing up because he was trying to conceal evidence or because he wanted a souvenir.

At 46 seconds, another shot reports. At 50 seconds another shot.

By Halloween night, I am so far gone that watching Lindeman die has degenerated into a philosophic exercise – into a rumination on the nature of truth.

I have become the English actor David Hemmings in Antonioni's 1966 film *Blow-Up*. Only I am without the soundtrack by Herbie Hancock and the Yardbirds, without the young and naked Vanessa Redgrave to distract me. I have Trick or Treaters at my door. I am wearing a tee shirt with a picture of a skeleton riding a rigid. I try not to scare the little ones.

In *Blow-Up*, Hemmings character is a man searching for the pixel thin line between fantasy and truth. He takes a photo of a couple screwing in a London park. When he enlarges the photo he sees a body in the bushes near the couple and he assigns himself the task of finding the truth, of solving this apparent murder. Eventually, after many blowups and many filter enhancements, after much staring at blurry images through a magnifying glass, he finally manages to see a hand holding a gun. Or is it a gun?

Over and over I go to my door and I say, "Don't you look cute. Now take turns. Happy Halloween!" And, then I go back to watching the last four seconds of John Lindeman's life and the two seconds immediately after it ends.

At 40 seconds John Lindeman's right arm seems to be held straight out from his body. He is just coming into view behind the orange interior wall of the QuikTrip. I cannot prove it, I might very well be wrong, but it seems to me that by then Ripley Lindeman is all alone.

If I am right, by then the A.R.M. who threw the first punch has been beaten to the ground. And, then he rose, thought about returning to the fight, recognized the gun fire and ran for his life. If I am right, Brad Lutzow has already been mortally wounded in or near his pickup truck. If I am right, Lindeman is now fighting alone. What he is fighting for I do not know.

I have been told that there were two guns involved in this murder, a 40 millimeter and a nine. I know Lindeman was shot four times. I do not exactly go play golf with the detective in charge of the case so I cannot ask him if Lindeman's hands were bagged.

At 40 seconds into the video John Ripley Lindeman is running straight at the Sober Rider who kills him. He is not running away. He is not running for his life. He is running toward his fate. The two men seem to be eight feet apart and Lindeman's right arm is extended. I cannot see anything in his hand. And then, after much staring at a blurry image I can. Or, maybe I can't.

If I had to guess, I would say that the most common firearms carried by bikers are the North American Arms, five shot, .22 caliber revolver, several brands (such as the Davis) of .22 caliber derringers and some flavor of .38 caliber derringer. None of them are shootout guns. All of them are "Lord, please lead me out of this bar" pistols. If you are reading this now you, yourself may own one of these excellent, disposable handguns. So, you know they are all pistols that are only effective at distances of six feet or less.

Certainly there must be a reason why John Lindeman fearlessly chased his killer across that parking lot. There must have been some reason why his killer was backing up. I cannot see a gun in Lindeman's hand but he might be holding a tiny gun like a derringer. And simultaneously, everything I have heard about Ripley

Lindeman in the past eight months leads me to believe that he was not a man who carried a gun. He was not a man who believed he had a reason to carry a gun.

I have to wonder, if Lindeman is holding a gun where did it come from? Is it a baby nine? A little nine can disappear in a man's hand, too. Is it the gun that fatally wounded Brad Lutzow? Did Lindeman take it off one of the killers?

Is he even holding a gun or is Lindeman only holding up his hand in a defensive gesture? Is he trying to grab the gun from his killers hand? I do not know. I am fairly certain the police know. But I do not cooperate with the police so they do not cooperate with me.

It is nine o'clock on the night of banshees and goblins and ghosts and hauntings and I am still watching video of a man who died months ago when the doorbell rings.
"Well aren't you sweet! Ooh! You scared me there, little partner! Happy Halloween!"

I go back to a computer screen so that over and over I can watch six seconds of video. There are three shots in quick succession. At 41 seconds into the tape Lindeman has been mortally wounded and his momentum is carrying him forward as he falls. He turns to his left as he falls. His killer gracefully dances out of the way so as not to get any of Lindeman's blood on his shoe.

Quickly the killer scampers around Lindeman and steps to the exact spot where Lindeman started to fall. The killer bends over and picks something off the ground. Then he disappears into the gloom.

Inside the store the clerk says, "Damn!"

And, if you have read this far, if you have been patient enough with me to have done that, if you are a normal person, if you are not me, you may have begun to wonder why I watched this one death over and over. I know it is a strange way to scribble out one's days.

And all I can tell you in my own defense, in John Lindeman's defense, is that every man dies twice. The first time he dies he becomes a corpse. And, the second time he dies he becomes forgotten.

A century ago, John Masefield, the longtime Poet Laureate of Britain wrote a sonnet about this second death. The corpse "cannot lift the silly hand again," Masefield declares in line three.

> *Nor speak, nor sing, it neither sees nor hears.*
> *And muffled mourners put it in the ground*
> *And then go home, and in the earth it lies,*
> *Too dark for vision and too deep for sound,*
> *The million cells that made a good man wise.*
> *Yet for a few short years an influence stirs*
> *A sense or wraith or essence of him dead,*
> *Which makes insensate things its ministers*
> *To those beloved, his spirit's daily bread;*
> *Then that, too, fades; in book or deed a spark*
> *Lingers, then that, too, fades; then all is dark.*

Life goes on without John Lindeman. But he died so fearlessly. The least I can do for him is cup my hands around his fading spark.

The Poker Run

Where you are going is always where you are. The destination is always the getting there.

So at the end of all my journeys it is 45 degrees and gray. I am sitting all alone at a red light on an empty stretch of Pacific Coast Highway. There is not a cop in sight so I could go anytime but I would rather watch gulls dance like mean drunks – just down there over the imaginary line between land and sea, between wet and dry, between the crashing and the still.

Then the end is Aviation Boulevard where the United States once had an aviation industry. Then the line where Aviation crosses Rosecrans.

Rosecrans is named for a Civil War hero who died along here someplace. The spot is unmarked. Rosecrans replaced a less heroic general named Buell. He was almost Lincoln's Vice-President in 1864 so he almost was President. But instead Rosecrans became the street that connects high crime Compton with recession proof Manhattan Beach.

Then the end is the 180 degree onramp to the 405, to the 105, past the Watts Towers to the roller coaster turn that becomes the 605 to the 10 which connects Santa Monica and the 5 with Jacksonville and the I-95.

I once rode a highly modified Sportster with a peanut tank so I know it is just over sixty miles from the Pacific to the TA Truck Stop in Ontario. Just as soon as the National Academy of Scooter Trash accepts my application I intend to nominate the TA Truck Stop in Ontario for the Biker Hall of Fame. This is the California biker motherland. The Run to the Wall used to start at that truck stop. For all I know it still does.

A couple of miles down the road is Fontana where the Hells Angels decided to call themselves that. And right next to Fontana is Bloomington which long ago, after the last good war, was full of Pissed Off Bastards – before all the Pissed Off Bastards moved to Berdoo. About 75 miles inland, just off a stretch of paint shaker road that nobody will ever smooth, is a roadhouse named Angels. It used to be called the Crossroads. And, just as soon as I get accepted, I am going to nominate Angels for the Hall of Fame, too.

Not everybody with twenty grand to spend on a motorcycle is willing to ride here. There is always too much traffic which always behaves as too much traffic always does. A maniac in a hybrid changes lanes frantically. He seems certain that he can find the opening everyone else has missed because he is smarter, better and, from the vantage of his climate controlled, soundproofed box, more environmentally aware than me. He cuts me off and stands on his brakes. I have seen him coming for miles. There is an accident a half mile ahead so he does not stay in front of me for long because I can split lanes. He cannot. And, I know he hates me for that. I know he would like to kill me over that. But, he does not kill me because I do not let him. By the time he imagines the lesson he should have taught that loud, obnoxious, aggressive biker I am already gone.

An ambulance pushes past me on the shoulder. It was a two car fight. One car lost a front wheel like a knocked-out tooth. I shudder and the bike shudders in my hands. Some day I will be on a stretch of road I know so well that I will be completely disarmed of fear. I will see the accident coming and I will accelerate hard to my left or my right to get as far away from the collision as I can. Then just out of the corner of my eye I will see something hurtling toward me. Maybe I will have time to understand I have been knocked over by a careening wheel. Maybe not. Then the cars behind me will run me over and that will be that.

So there goes the last of my happy mood. Now I am grumpy because sometimes I like to imagine I will live forever. For the next thirty or forty miles I am spooked by every little thing. A boxy, seventies pickup sheds trash like dandruff. A plastic water bottle escapes in slow motion. A sandwich bag floats like a feather. I always hate the trash that floats on the wind. I fly around him after a can pops out.

A half mile ahead of him a car drifts left then lurches right. I edge up next to the driver. Sometimes that is enough. They don't have to hear what I am screaming. They just have to know that I am crazy enough to do that. Just seeing me right there with my face contorted in senseless rage usually encourages them to put both hands on the wheel and look straight ahead. But this guy is so engrossed in rolling a joint on his lap that he never even notices that I am there. That is the third or fourth time I have seen that in the last couple of years. I used to think texters were bad.

As I speed away a little tumbler in my head goes click. Now I get it.

There is a music festival in Coachella, east of Palm Springs, all weekend so the worst of this traffic is music lovers. Many of them will be spending the night on site. So when traffic suddenly slows again and parts into lines I am not surprised to see a fallen sleeping bag. I actually ride as close to the bag as I can, just to show my contempt, about which nobody cares but me. Then by either pure, naked luck or the complexity of the Lord's plan I am maneuvering far over on the right when the sleeping bag's companion, a feather pillow, explodes into an instant blizzard and even I have to admit that all those feathers are pretty.

Another few minutes and I am past the first Indian casino and the born again dinosaurs of Cabazon and into the windmill forest when all four lanes are covered with what must have been two gross of dancing pastel thongs: Yellow, pink, teal, baby blue and fuchsia. I think the carton from which they escaped is over in lane one. I can tell these must be high quality thongs. They appear to be made of the finest, lightest, synthetic cloth. They tumble down the freeway in rolling waves. And that is the exact moment when I realize again, for the thousandth time, that it never matters where I am going. The thongs make me smile all the way to Indio and out into the emptiness beyond.

I like to ride the western deserts: The Mojave, the Great Basin and the Colorado. Whatever I am chasing I almost catch out there. Although this is not my favorite desert season. It has been a wet, *el nino* winter so the desert is green and full of tiny bugs. Sometimes they explode on my face and hands like sprinkles of rain and sometimes I feel like I am suffocating in clouds of them.

Around the fallen dream called Desert Center I overtake a truck trailing a long, burlap or muslin shroud. Some lumper has left this curtain outside the locked trailer doors and now most of the top has torn away and the bottom has twisted into a slowly breaking whip. Two or three times I swear the cloth has broken loose before I finally twist my right hand and fly around him and again I am practically alone. Just me and the desert and blue heaven and the bugs. This desert seems timeless – as free of history as people – but that is only an illusion like painter's perspective.

Chevron and a couple other corporations plan to build three solar generating plants out here in all this nothing. Reportedly, the twelve thousand mirrors will not cover the "Blythe intaglios," a collection of giant drawings scraped into the desert 4,000 years ago like the more famous Nazca lines in Peru.

The proper name for this kind of art is "geoglyph" and the really interesting ones out here are drawings of *Kokopelli* and *Cicimitl*. *Kokopelli* is the hump-backed flautist whose image is carved into rocks all over the Four Corners. All the really cool archaeologists think *Kokopelli* it is a representation of a new religion, called the *kachina* cult, that popped up about the time the builders of Chaco and Mesa Verde abandoned those cities and started moving south. Kokopelli might have been an historic person, or he might be representative of the merchants who moved parrots north from Mexico and jade and turquoise south. Or he might just have been the twelfth century equivalent of Bart Simpson. Nobody really knows. And, now people mostly worship Kokopelli in souvenir shops and tourist traps all over the west.

Cicimitl was sort of the Aztec Charon, who led lost souls to the underworld. And, neo-Aztecs drive out here from the cities to dance around *Kokopelli* and *Cicimitl*. And they worry that the new solar plants might cover them over. And this weird and zany convergence of the ancient and the future, of secret native sorcery and soulless corporate technology fascinates me.

Although it would fascinate me more if the *Kokopelli* and *Cicimitl* were truly ancient. The disillusioning truth is that they were not carved into the mother earth until around 1994. I mention them only because I like to think when I ride the less crowded roads. Out here I think about the geoglyphs. Even though I know that daydreaming represents exactly the kind of apathy that will kill you on a motorcycle. I dream anyway because I learned a long time ago that nobody lives forever.

I cross what is left of the Colorado at Blythe. This far down the river seven states have already drunk most of it. The thirstiest of them are California, Arizona and Nevada so here the river is, at most, a third as wide as it is at Laughlin 115 miles to the north. A mile past the river I spot the first groves of *saguaro*, the big cacti that look like a man waving hello. And about a mile past the first *saguaro* the traffic bunches and slows because a couple of Arizona Highway patrolmen are glaring at each passing vehicle and waving a gesture that simultaneously means slow down and giddy-up.

Arizona has always been a scatter of straws. It looks just like whatever you want. To me it looks like an hysterical, all-American, Mexican, wild west, futuristic police state.

The contradictions here are too numerous to list. Arizona was the last of the contiguous states to enter the Union in 1912 and before then there was some debate about whether the Arizona Territory was Democrat or Republican. It was the Republicans' idea to turn it into a state. All the small ranchers, and outlaws and cowboys and rustlers and dreamers in this desert were natural Democrats. All the big mine owners and land speculators and mercantilists were Republicans. The history of Arizona is the history of big time Republicans like the Goldwaters hiring small time Democrats like the Earps to shoot some sense into other small time Democrats like the Clantons.

Arizona was practically founded on rustling cattle down in old Mexico and selling them north of *la linea*. Now the same place is an uproar over all the entrepreneurs who are smuggling in drugs over those same, old desert trails. Of course, there is a war going on just down there. And, the great terror in Arizona is that the war will invade the north, again, just like Pancho Villa did during the last Mexican war. On television, they call it the "Battle for the Border" and it is a recurring segment on the evening news.

Arizona is getting ready. In Arizona, any felony free, citizen can carry a loaded pistol in his boot or in his pocket or tucked inside his jeans under his shirt. In another couple of months federal firearms laws will no longer apply to guns made and kept in Arizona. Hell, I have already given some thought to moving over here and opening up a little machine gun shop.

At the same time this is a state where you can get arrested just because a cop thinks you look Mexican. Not even Mexican. You can get arrested here on the suspicion that you look illegal. And the consequences of being arrested can be nasty.

The Maricopa County Sheriff is a mean, fat, loud man named Joe Arpaio. Arpaio plays "America's Toughest Sheriff" on reality TV. He abuses, humiliates and malnourishes any prisoner he can get his hands on. He houses them in tents in the desert summer, limits how much they can drink and if you talk back he will put you on a chain gang. And, most of working class, desperately broke Arizona adores and identifies with Sheriff Joe as it indentifies with angry *Fox News* and working class George W. Bush.

My favorite thing about Arizona is that I can ride helmet free. Arizona and I both agree that it is my head and I can adorn or unadorn it as I wish.

A few miles past the scowling cops simultaneously telling me to slow down and get along I run through my least favorite thing – a "photo enforcement zone." That's what they call them here. They are robot, fine collecting machines and they are part of Arizona's master plan to survive. Turning Arizona into the neo-Alamo is going to cost a lot of money. And, now that this territory has run out of most of its silver, copper and gold; now that most of those free cattle down in Mexico are gone; now that the water is running low the Arizona economy is more dependent than ever on the traffic ticket industry.

What kind of puzzles me is why more people don't just pull their pistols out of their boots and shoot these pernicious machines. I might have done that myself except I was going about ninety at the time, passing a truck, and I didn't see the thing until it was already too late.

I stop for gas in Quartzite and then again in Tonopah. I drive around Phoenix on the 101 Beltway and eventually, 405 miles from the coast, I pull into a gas station on Bell Road. I can barely hear the guy who asks me, "Is there some kind of a run today?"

Mostly I hear my motorcycle, even with the engine turned off. I think I say, "Yep." That's what I intend to say. I don't actually know if any sound came out of my mouth or not.

I pull out of the station and find my way into the shopping center across the street. Near the northeast corner is a lot full of motorcycles and a crowded bar called the Steel Horse Saloon. I park and go pay my money for the poker run.

Poker runs are sort of the American biker equivalent of a scavenger hunt. You find your way from place to place, get your ticket punched and in the end the resulting pattern of holes on a piece of cardboard gets translated into a five card poker hand.

The poker run was invented by a hot rod club called the Mid-Cal Stockers in Lodi, California in March 1950. For a few years after the Second World War the club ran "rallies" every Spring. The idea of the rally was to run a race without actually breaking the speed limit so the courses were controlled and difficult to navigate. In 1950 the Stockers decided to spice things up. Drivers had to decide at each of five control points whether to turn left or right. If they guessed correctly they got a card. That gave everybody two chances to win. Even if you did not win the rally you could still win the "poker run." The Stockers handed out the prizes that night at a "bean feed" at the clubhouse of the Lodi Women's Motorcycle Club. That was how these things got started. As soon as organizers decided to pass out the cards in bars the idea was perfected.

This poker run is sponsored by the Cave Creek Charter of the Hells Angels and it is intended to celebrate the beginning of Sonny Barger's 54th year in the club.

I will never live long enough to know for sure, but I think Barger is one of those American frontier figures that pop up every hundred years. They are characters that America invents over and over because without them and the masculine ideals they represent there can no longer be an America. And America has chosen these particular men because in a certain light, remembered in a certain way, at certain times they have actually managed to be exactly who we all need them to be. Lives fly past but myths persist.

The first of these great frontier heroes was a man named Daniel Boone. He was born about 200 years before Barger. He lived to be 85. And six years after he died the American novelist James Fennimore Cooper wrote a book about him called *The Last of the Mohicans*. Until it was banished by the counter-culture the novel was part of the American canon. It is the tale of a self sufficient, resourceful, brave man overcoming red demons and the wilderness to rescue his kidnapped daughter. Every educated young American man was supposed to know it – as much as anything for its portrait of what an American man should be. Even now, the story retains the power to excite the American soul. Michael Mann directed the last movie version of it in 1992.

The last real, geographic frontier, the Old West, disappeared in and into serial episodes. The Silver Rush started in Tombstone in 1879. Doc Holliday died in 1887. John Wesley Harding was killed in 1895. Butch Cassidy and the Sundance Kid moved to New York in 1902. A year later, a former Edison cameraman named Edwin S. Porter made the first movie Western – in New York City. The Yukon Gold Rush came and went in 1897. The last frontier hero, Wyatt Earp, went north that year to run a card game in Alaska. Earp died in the first fortnight of 1929 in Los Angeles. His pall bearers included the Western movie stars Tom Mix and William S. Hart. According to a mourner named Adella Rogers St. John, Tom Mix broke down and wept.

Barger became a public figure about thirty-five years after that. His first biographer, Hunter Thompson wrote in 1965: "In any gathering of Hells Angels, from five to a possible hundred and fifty, there is no doubt who is running the show: Ralph 'Sonny' Barger, the Maximum Leader, a six-foot, 170-pound warehouseman from East Oakland, the coolest head in the lot, and a tough, quick-thinking dealer when any action starts. By turns he is a fanatic, a philosopher, a brawler, a shrewd compromiser and a final arbitrator. To the Oakland Angels he is Ralph. Everybody else calls him Sonny...."

For all these years, Barger has had to live with that. He has already had almost as long a run as Earp. In a book published last year, ATF Agent Jay Dobyns gushed about meeting Barger:

"This was the first time I'd laid eyes on the man. He was around sixty-five, but looked to have the health of a vibrant man in his mid-fifties, a remarkable achievement considering the paces he's put his body through over the decades.... For those who don't know, this was the man – the legend, really – who molded the Hells Angels into what they are. It's not a stretch to say that Sonny Barger is a visionary who essentially created the image of the outlaw biker as we know it."

Now, on top of everything else, Barger has to live with that.

He cannot just be one of us. He has to carry the burden of epitomizing all of us. I have heard him praised by people who hate his club. The very best thing about Sonny Barger may be that he carries the burden cheerfully.

Probably a third of all American men can describe him. In person he looks younger than he photographs. He looks to me the same way he has always looked. He looks like Dennis the Menace grown old. I am certain that he must have a walk-in closet full of sleeveless tee shirts and blue jeans that are neither too new nor too shabby.

He has to know he is the biggest star in America. I don't know how he lives with it. He is everything that a once in each century American hero should be. He is himself. And whoever that is, is close enough to the myth most of America still wants to believe. He is gracious, confidant and surrounded by men who would die for him. And, most astounding of all, there is not a paparazzo in sight. I think I spot two under cover cops. I think they are cops because they are the only people I see who look nervous.

So that moment leaning on my bike fifteen feet away from him, wondering if he might actually outlive me, knowing that I can only write about him, that he will never write about me is the end. And watching the lot slowly fill is another end.

I push into the bar, buy a bottle of water and come back to the bike to drink. A skinny brunette asks to take my picture and I tell her sure. I give her a slightly hard time and then I tell her sure. She has already clicked the shudder before I tell her she can. So somewhere out there is a picture of a guy with a mustache, in a flannel shirt, aviator sunglasses and a black beanie leaning a dusty Dyna and that is one of the scattered, little pieces that might survive me.

Eventually the bikes begin to growl. The way the Cave Creek Angels run a poker run is everybody travels from bar to bar in a pack.

The pack lines up, jostles and begins to spill out onto Bell. The front of the pack has probably reached Interstate 17 when I turn onto the street. At least half the pack is still behind me. Once the first bikes hit the freeway everyone behind must speed up. Nobody cares about red lights. Nobody gives a damn about photo enforcement zones. Laws and controls are irrelevant because we are all Americans. We are natural and free and in a saddle which is just where we were born to be.

We force ourselves onto the freeway the way bold men force coy women. Some cars are smart enough to let us have our way and some are not. I twist open the throttle and try to catch the front of the pack. Everybody is trying to do the same thing.

I glance down at my speedometer just long enough to see I am somewhere north of 90. And I laugh. Because, I don't give a damn who remembers me. And because, if I am ever made to choose, this is just how I would choose to die.

23418768R00175

Made in the USA
Middletown, DE
25 August 2015